Dear Educator,

Teach that young Black male that for every enemy, there is a friend. Teach him that for every scoundrel there is a hero, that for every crooked politician, there is a dedicated leader. Teach him that a dollar earned is better than a hundred dollars stolen. Teach him it is far more honorable to fail than to cheat. Teach him how to gracefully lose, and enjoy winning when he does win. Teach him to be gentle with people and tough with tough people. Steer him away from envy and teach him the secret of quiet laughter. Teach him how to laugh when he is sad, teach him there is no shame in tears. Teach him there can be glory in failure and despair in success. Teach him to scoff at cynics.

Teach him the wonders of a good book, but also give time to explore the mysteries of the world. Teach him to have faith in his own ideas, even if everyone tells him he is crazy. Try to help him understand the strength in not following the crowd. Teach him to sell his talents and brains to the highest bidder but never to sell his soul. Let him have the courage to be impatient, let him have the patient to be brave. Teach him to have unwavering faith in himself. Teach him that for every enemy, there is a friend.

Thank you for all that you have done this far in your career. Thank you for choosing the path to becoming a teacher. Thank you for your hard work and dedication to the children of the future. Thank you for your kindness and patience towards our children. Thank you for being a positive influence. I'm here to tell you that I appreciate you; your hard work, dedication, and patience with our children.

Other Books by the Author

Books available at www.craigboykin

(THE I.E.P. TRAP)
Copyright © 2023 by (Craig J. Boykin)

All rights reserved. No part of this book may be reproduced or transmitted in any form or by any means without written permission from the author.

Printed in USA by 48HrBooks (www.48HrBooks.com)

Table of Contents

About the Author: 6

Introduction: 8

Chapter 1:　Trapped in History　21

Chapter 2:　The Media Trap　37

Chapter 3:　Trapped in Soft Bigotry　47

Chapter 4:　Stress Trap　71

Chapter 5:　Sympathy Trap　93

Chapter 6:　Trapped in Inequality　103

Chapter 7:　Trapped in The Pipeline　111

Chapter 8:　Trapped in The Gaps　137

Conclusion:　Trapped in Black Skin　144

Bibliography　159

About the Author

Craig J. Boykin has made a name for himself speaking nationally with his unapologetically REAL approach to systemic poverty and trauma. Craig doesn't mind speaking the hard truth. He is a seven-time author and decorated Army veteran. Craig's self-made success comes from his hustle, his grit and his relentless desire to never give up. Raised by a single mother who was addicted to drugs. Craig grew up without his father and no clear path to success. He repeated the 3rd & 5th grade and was diagnosed with a learning disability, and placed in SPED. Traumatized and confused, Craig became a very problematic student and was kicked out of school often. Craig ultimately dropped out of high school in the 10th grade.

While writing the I.E.P Trap. Craig kept researching an alarming stat that didn't sit very well with him. Less than two percent of educators are black males. After consulting for 10 plus years, Craig took a 7th grade career explorations position at one of the most challenging middle schools in Montgomery, Alabama. Most professional speakers leave education to consult full time, Craig transitioned from consulting full time to a full-time educator. If that doesn't speak to the validity of his heart I don't know what does.

Today, although Craig is in the trench's day in and day out he continues to electrifies audiences and delivers an incredibly inspiring and actionable presentation. Craig has coined the phrase GED to PhD. Craig is a master storyteller, people are drawn in immediately to Craig and the essence of his message. Craig has worked with a myriad of diverse companies including keynoting at Harvard University and the keynote for the 50th Anniversary of the civil rights in Washington D.C. during Barack Obama's presidency. Craig is changing the narrative of high school dropouts in his family, He is the definition of a "True Underdog."

Introduction

This world is forever changing and those who fail to change with it fall behind. It's unfortunate to say, but the current state of public education is sort of right, largely wrong, and fatally imprecise. Many would argue that it's broken, I would say that its actually brilliantly constructed just not for the 21st century student. Decades ago, the educational system was designed to meet the new demands of industrial revolution. The establishment of large manufacturing companies created new demands.

This brought about the invention of new machinery and new farming techniques as well as the invention of new technology, which in turn led to mass industrialization. The industrial revolution also brought about several changes to the educational system. Some negative, most were positive. Some of the most notable changes to the educational system include:

Establishment of Training Schools:

The mass growth of industries from textile to energy-based saw the need for more competent workers to work in the factories and manufacturing plants. It brought about the need to have schools to train people on how to work with the newly invented machinery. Many training schools were established all around Europe and America.

Specialization in Careers:

Before the industrial revolution, students were only taught the basic arithmetic concepts. However, this era brought the need to specialize in different fields of profession. It allowed people to choose a profession in which to specialize. Some of the earliest industrial specialization fields are: Textile industry, Energy production, and the Medical field.

Mandatory Education for All:

Education was made compulsory for all children up to the age of ten. This meant that every child, whether from an affluent or poor background, had a chance to access an education. Before the industrial revolution, only children from wealthy families were afforded the luxury of getting an education. It changed after and became inclusive to all.

Women Were Allowed to Access an Education:

During the Industrial Revolution, women were also allowed to access an education. However, education was still based on different gender roles that saw women learn lessons like cookery, needlework, and housewifery. One, however, cannot fail to recognize that it was a step in the right direction for gender equality in education.

Establishment of Higher Institutes of Learning:

Apart from teaching the basic elementary skills of how to read and write, higher institutions of learning were also established. They mostly dealt with specialized fields and led to the rise of highly qualified experts that would continue inventing new technologies.

Increased Government Support on Education:

In Britain, the government became more involved in the education sector by using more funds to ensure that its citizens were literate. As a result, many schools developed and libraries were established for people to access information easily.

Child Labor:

It's a shortcoming that came with the Industrial revolution. The government allowed children to work in the industries despite them being too young to work and untrained. This meant that the children were exploited and paid minimal wages for the work they did. To curb this, the government made it compulsory for industries to provide a 2-hour training.

Training of Teachers:

Colleges were also established to train teachers to be employed in the new schools. The increase in a number of tutors led to an increase in the number of learners in the institutions. It is a move that improved literacy levels in Europe and America.

During the Industrial Revolution factory owners needed docile workers who would show up on time and do what they were told. Sitting in a classroom all day with a teacher was good training for that. "Factory schools," as they are now called, originated in early 19th century Prussia. For the first time, education was provided by the state and learning was regimented.

Dozens of students at a time were placed in grades according to their age, and moved through successive grades as they mastered the curriculum. They took an industrialized approach to education: impersonal, efficient, and standardized. Much of this education, however, was not technical in nature but social and moral. Workers who had always spent their working days in a domestic setting, had to be taught to follow orders, to respect the space and property rights of others, be punctual, docile, and sober.

The transition to factory work was unpleasant, to put it mildly. The idea that men had to show up and take orders from a boss of whom they were not even related to was demeaning and emasculating. Factory conditions were often terrible and completely changed how people organized their days. Time was no longer their own.

The industrial revolution ended in the early 1900's and sadly the educational system hasn't changed much since. It's the 21st century, and teachers are still using what is often referred to as the Factory Model. The Factor Model should've been obsolete decades ago, but somehow, it's still very much in operation well into what is progressively becoming a world propelled by the internet and technology. Another outdated commonly used method that educators still use in education is the "cemetery method." This method is a reference to the practice of arranging classrooms similar to cemeteries. All the students are in rows, very still and very quiet.

That may have been the established standard for students when the workforce needed bodies who were on time, obedient and able to perform monotonous tasks. They didn't need, nor want creative thinkers and free minds. The students were being trained, not educated.

In his book, The Global Achievement Gap, Tony Wagner of Harvard University articulated what he calls the 7 Survival Skills for the 21st Century. Many of these skills were not considered desirable for students or workers during the Industrial Revolution. However, in the 21st century these skills are absolutely critical for students to succeed.

1. ***Critical Thinking and Problem Solving***
2. ***Collaboration across Networks and Leading by Influence***
3. ***Agility and Adaptability***
4. ***Initiative and Entrepreneurialism***
5. ***Effective Oral and Written Communication***
6. ***Accessing and Analyzing Information***
7. ***Creativity and Imagination***

Rate these 7 Survival Skills students will need the 21st Century from 1 (most used) to 7 (least used) during a school day by your students.

1.	
2.	
3.	
4.	
5.	
6.	
7.	

Now, how can you as an educator improve on 3,4,5,6, and 7 from day to day in your classroom.

"What do I mean when I talk about transformational productivity reforms that can also boost student outcomes? Our K–12 system largely still adheres to the century-old, industrial-age factory model of education. A century ago, maybe it made sense to adopt seat-time requirements for graduation and pay teachers based on their educational credentials and seniority. Educators were right to fear the large class sizes that prevailed in many schools. But the factory model of education is the wrong model for the 21st century."

US Secretary of Education Arne Duncan (2010)

Critical Thinking & Problem Solving

Students will apply knowledge and skills in practical ways to solve real world problems. The teacher provides the activities, experiences, and feedback needed for students to develop critical thinking and problem-solving skills.

Initiative & Entrepreneurship

Students will be self-directed in determining ways to seek out new opportunities' ideas, and strategies for improvement. Teachers will create a student-centered classroom that provides multiple opportunities for students to be self-directed learners.

Effective Oral & Written Communication

Students will be able to communicate their thoughts clearly and precisely through energy, passion and authentic voice.

Collaboration Across Networks and Leading by Influence

Students need the ability to learn and work fluidly understanding how collaboration can be most effective and where their skills can most influence the learning task.

Agility and Adaptability

In a 21st century classroom, students will think, be flexible and adaptable to change while using a variety of tools to solve problems. Students will understand that there can be multiple solutions to a problem. The teacher will ensure that students receive instruction designed to elicit innovative and creative thinking and problem solving.

Accessing and Analyzing Information

Accessing and analyzing information is the ability to know when there is a need for information and how to identify, locate, evaluate and effectively use that information for solving problems. In the 21st Century classroom, students find, navigate through, and evaluate large amounts of information. Teachers provide guided and independent research opportunities for students to make informed decisions and create products.

Curiosity and Imagination

Curiosity and imagination are the capacity to synthesize existing ideas and to work creatively in ways characterized by innovation and divergent thinking. In the 21 Century classroom, students develop original ideas and create products by applying critical thinking, research methods, communication tools and collaborative processes. Teachers provide experiences that allow students to create unique ideas and products.

1983 was a pivotal year for the technology industry. Microsoft released MS Word and Apple introduced the new Apple IIe (a series of personal computers produced by Apple Computer). Many experts predicted that the demand for better schools, coupled with the supply of computers and new software, would soon revolutionize Americas classrooms.

It didn't quite happen. Schools did make attempts to adopt new technologies, computers and software. They increased bandwidth, and infrastructure. But there is little research-based evidence that these tools have had the exponential impact on public education that many anticipated. This seems unreal given the enormous impact that technology has had on nearly every other aspect of the world, how can that be? Well maybe that's because we have incorporated new age technology within a school structure that is virtually unchanged since the mid-nineteenth century.

Superintendents, educators, consultants, publishers, business professionals, and corporations all strongly believe that bringing in the latest technologies makes a classroom "21st century". It is completely possible that the school has all the latest technologies and they are still operating under the old factory model. The teacher is just doing it digitally instead of with paper and pencil. 21st century students cannot become self-directed, independent, collaborative, problem-solving, and entrepreneurial if they are spending their days in teacher centered classrooms arranged in rows. Even those classrooms where the students are in groups the teacher centered paradigm still prevails. Students acquire these skills through opportunities to practice these skills, not by being passive recipients of lectures.

"Students brain activity is virtually non-existent during lectures, even lower than when they are asleep. Lectures equal brain "flatlining."

Professor **Rosalind *W*. Picard**

The ideal 21st century learning environment would provide spaces for students to learn independently and collaboratively in groups small or large. At this point everyone is frustrated, standardized test scores are down, and student disrespect is at an all-time high. Students are basically over the factory model way of teaching. They know better! Research has shown that students drop out simply because school is boring, and they see unquestionably no relevance in it.

Real Question: Have you ever asked your students if your teaching style is boring? What did they say? Did you make any changes? Were you offended? Do your students understand the relevance of the subject matter you are teaching in regard to their future? Is your subject matter really relevant to their future?

Public education has become nothing more than test prep centers; perhaps test prep factories is more accurate. Teachers' jobs are to ensure that these students memorize as many facts as possible, as quickly as possible, and hopefully remember all this for the test. Basically, we are force-feeding students' discrete bits of information, with no regard as to their interests, skills, experiences or even the fact that they are human beings and not machines.

Emotional Trauma and the Hippocampus

The hippocampus is part of the limbic system in the brain. It is mostly responsible for storing and retrieving memories. Trauma may leave the hippocampus physically affected; studies have shown that people suffering from trauma usually have a smaller hippocampus than others. So, students who have experienced trauma are at a disadvantage in today's "remember this" and "regurgitate it back" to me on a test public-schooling learning environment.

Trapped in History

Ch. 1

"Those who do not learn history are doomed to repeat it." The quote is most likely from writer and philosopher George Santayana, and in its original form it read, "Those who cannot remember the past are condemned to repeat it." America has a dark history of segregation and inequality in public education. Public education seems to be divided into two different systems. General education and special education. In a perfect world they would work cohesively together to meet the needs of all learners but let's be honest, it hardly happens.

It's hard to change a system that was set up to separate learners in the first place. The segregation of students with disabilities, like the segregation of Black students, has an ugly history in America, and the effects continue to linger into the 21st century. The 1954 Brown v. Board of Education ruling paved the way for the 1975 federal law (now called the Individuals with Disabilities

Education Act) which required schools to give students with disabilities access to a quality education.

In Topeka, KS there's a national historic site for the Brown v. Board. The first thing one would see when they enter the historic site is a plaque inscribed with these famous words from the U.S. Supreme Court's 1954 ruling: "We conclude that in the field of public education the doctrine of 'separate but equal' has no place. Separate educational facilities are inherently unequal." More than four decades later, in the landmark 1999 decision in Olmstead v. L.C., the Court made essentially the same point about the institutionalization of people with disabilities, ruling that this practice amounts to a discriminatory and unjust form of segregation, in violation of Title II of the Americans with Disabilities Act.

Segregation according to a person's race in the United States has been declared illegal since the 1950s, however the numbers would indicate that public schools are still very much segregated in the 21st century. In 2004, Congress reauthorized the Individuals with

Disabilities Education Act (IDEA) because it reported disturbing findings: an "intensification of problems connected with mislabeling high dropout rates among minority children with disabilities."

Congress elaborated:

"More minority children continue to be served in special education than would be expected from the percentage of minority students in the general school population. African-American children are identified as having intellectual disabilities and emotional disturbance at rates greater than their white counterparts. In the 1998-99 school year, African-American children represented just 14.8 percent of the population aged 6 through 21, but comprised 20.2 percent of all children with disabilities. Studies have found that schools with predominately white students and teachers have placed disproportionately high numbers of their minority students into special education."

Gary Orfield, co-director of the Civil Rights Project at Harvard University, said racial inequities have become so pervasive that no school district can afford to be smug about it.

"One of the things our study suggests is that nobody should be assuming that racial inequity in special education is somebody else's problem until they look at their own data," Orfield said. "We really see it everywhere we look. It's happening lots of places that have a progressive image."

Let's trace this country's unacceptable history of segregation and racism in education and examining how it has affected Black students from coast to coast.

19th century: By the 1830s, most southern states in the U.S. had passed legislation that forbade teaching enslaved people how to read. Those who became literate did so at significant risk. But by 1865, after the end of the Civil War, more and more Blacks then referred to as African Americans were putting pressure on Republicans to update state constitutions to provide free, public education to Black children.

Still, Jim Crow law a collection of legislation that emerged once the U.S. Constitution abolished slavery aimed to control just about every aspect of Black Americans' livelihood. In 1896, the U.S. Supreme Court ruled on Plessy v. Ferguson. By confirming Louisiana's right to "separate but equal" railroad cars in this landmark case, the federal government set a precedent that legalized segregation. Soon after, southern states began passing laws mandating segregation in public schools.

1930-1950: Between 1930 and 1950, the National Association for the Advancement of Colored People (NAACP) began to sue over unequal pay for Black educators. This, plus the realization that more and more Black labor was moving north to urban areas, helped to increase spending in some southern, Black schools.

1950-1960: By 1954, the Supreme Court had ruled on Brown vs. Board of Education of Topeka. In the ruling, which overturned Plessy v. Ferguson, the Supreme Court admitted that "separate education facilities are inherently unequal." Unfortunately, the idea of desegregation was met with resistance. For example, in Virginia, the state enacted the Stanley Plan legislation designed to slash state funding for integrated schools.

Aimed at avoiding integration, this approach enabled white families to enroll their children in private, segregated schools with the help of tuition grants. This resulted in public school districts being closed. Items that belonged to the now-shuttered public schools were physically relocated to the private, segregated schools.

In 1957, Arkansas Governor Orval Faubus sent the state's National Guard to stop nine Black students known as "the Little Rock Nine" from enrolling in a formerly white high school. Eventually, President Eisenhower sent federal troops to enforce the desegregation. (It's important to note, however, that Eisenhower was not a staunch civil rights supporter; he intervened mainly because he wanted to demonstrate that a state could not use military power to defy federal orders.)

1960-1970s: In 1960, Ruby Bridges became the first black student at her New Orleans elementary school. She also, however, became the only student. The parents of all the other children in the school pulled them out of class in protest. In 1964, The Civil Rights Act was signed into law. Famously, the legislation prohibits discrimination based on race, sex, religion and nationality.

By 1966, the Coleman Report revealed the benefits of Black students attending integrated schools, emphasizing the future importance of "busing" to desegregate public schools further. By 1971, Swann v. Charlotte-Mecklenburg Board of Education upheld "busing" as the best solution to "racial imbalances" at schools. A 1974 Supreme Court ruling, however, set progress back a step when Miliken v. Bradley effectively legalized segregation by refusing to desegregate *between* school districts. This created inherent segregation between urban school districts that served Black families and the wealthy, suburban school districts that served white families.

1990-2000: In the mid to late '90s, educational legislation in California was making headlines. First, in 1996, the Oakland School District proposed declaring Ebonics the native language of Black students. This was seen as an attempt to secure more funding for effectively segregated Black schools. The same year, the state passed Proposition 209, which rendered affirmative action in public employment, contracting and education illegal. A year later, the proposition was overturned federally.

2000-2023: By 2001, the No Child Left Behind Act (NCLB) was ratified. This legislation aimed to hold schools accountable for student performance by withholding funds from schools that did not make adequate progress toward NCLB's goals. Still widely viewed as controversial, the legislation was replaced by Every Student Succeeds Act in 2015.

Today, studies show that while students across the country are growing more diverse, public schools are still effectively segregated to some extent. In fact, a 2022 report issued by the U.S. Government Accountability Office (GAO) indicated that more than one-third of American students attended a school whose student body was predominantly of the same race.

Experts agree that historical efforts to keep neighborhoods segregated including "redlining" continue to affect the makeup of schools today. This is especially true in areas where most students attend their local public schools. Experts also concede that "district secession," which occurs when a locality departs from a larger school district, has contributed to ongoing segregation in schools.

Finally, while the coronavirus pandemic affected all students across the country, certain groups were hit hardest. According to a McKinsey report on learning loss, school shutdowns exacerbated racial disparities. Data shows that students of color fell farther behind in learning during the pandemic, and were likelier to return to in-person learning later.

IEP's were first introduced into the school system in the mid 1970's, they were to ensure that students with a documented disability whether it be a learning or physical, had the right to a quality education also. As recent as 1970 in the U.S., American schools only educated one in five children with disabilities, and many states had laws rejecting certain students, including children who identified as: deaf, blind, emotionally disturbed, or had an intellectual disability. Fast forward 50 years and we now have a serious over-representation of Black males in special education. Black males are subject to disparities in SPED identification and discipline practices.

Have you ever encountered a student that was labeled SPED but it was obvious that this student wasn't in need of SPED services? If you have been in education for more than two days, I am sure you have. Here is the real question, what did you do about it?

In general, significant disproportionality can lead to poor academic outcomes for black males. Isn't it ironic that five of the seven states today with the highest over-representation of black males in SPED are southern states where the races were once separated by law: Mississippi, Alabama, North Carolina, South Carolina, and Florida.

The disproportionate representation of Black males in SPED is a symptom of a much larger problem in America, which funnels Black male students into separate classrooms (self-contained) at extremely high rates and if most educators was being totally honest they conceivably wouldn't care, as long as it gets that problem out of their class. Any time a label is placed on anyone particularly a susceptible child, the likelihood of that child feeling different increases.

The problem of minority overrepresentation in special education is particularly troubling, because of the growing use of tests that burden poorly taught children with diploma denial and grade level retention. One study suggests that the inappropriate reliance on high-stakes testing likely exacerbates the consistent problem of the exclusion of low achieving and special education students from state assessments used for school and district accountability. Two of the reports also suggest that inappropriate and inadequate special education services may be a leading factor in overrepresentation of minority adolescents in the juvenile justice system.

A SPED classroom 20 years ago was comprised of students the educational system deemed as "retarded." Mental retardation was a term commonly used 20 years ago. However, over time the term "retard" has morphed into a derogatory insult. The term is now universally considered offensive and, in most cases, it is frowned upon. In 2010 President Obama signed Rosa's Law.

The law removed the term "mental retardation" from federal education, health and labor statutes, replacing it with "intellectual disability." The law was named for Rosa Marcellino, a young woman with Down syndrome whose family engaged in a two-year campaign to change the terminology. In a White House ceremony,

President Obama echoed the words of Nick Marcellino, Rosa's teenage brother, who said,

"What you call people is how you treat them. If we change the words, maybe it will be the start of a new attitude toward people with disabilities."

In the 21st century we now know there are various degrees of disabilities that may impact how a student learns. Between 2000 and 2010, the number of kids with autism more than tripled. Which sparked the demand for even more special education intervention and professionals.

It's no secret that Black males are more likely than any other group to be placed in special education classes. On the other end of the extreme, Black males are also less likely to be classified as "gifted and talented" even if their academic record shows that potential.

How many Black males have you recommended for SPED over your educational career? Now, how many have you recommended for the gifted program?

If all things were considered equally, these statistics would indicate that there is something genetically wrong with Black males that is causing a higher frequency of disabilities and reduced percentage of gifted referrals.

However, we know better. While some, perhaps even a majority, of the Black males categorized as SPED belong in that grouping, some are simply misunderstood and misplaced due to unaddressed behavior and trauma issues.

Exposure to chronic, prolonged traumatic experiences has the potential to alter children's brains, which may cause longer-term effects in areas such as:

Students have Attachment issues: Trouble with relationships, boundaries, empathy, and social isolation.

Physical Health: Impaired sensorimotor development, coordination problems, increased medical problems, and somatic symptoms.

Emotional Regulation: Difficulty identifying or labeling feelings and communicating needs.

Dissociation: Altered states of consciousness, amnesia, impaired memory.

Cognitive Ability: Problems with focus, learning, processing new information, language development, planning and orientation to time and space.

33

Self-Concept: Lack of consistent sense of self, body image issues, low self-esteem, shame and guilt.

Behavioral Control: Difficulty controlling impulses, oppositional behavior, aggression, disrupted sleep and eating patterns, trauma re-enactment.

While unpleasant behavior is certainly a symptom of learning disabilities like ADHD and some degrees of autism it isn't itself a disability. A lack of understanding surrounding how Black males navigate in this world, and a quick trigger when it comes to disciplinary and removal practices, is a recipe for higher than average numbers. This is not something that we as any educators can and/or should sit by and let continue.

A large body of research shows that inclusive educational settings, in contrast with segregated classrooms, provide many benefits for students with disabilities, including increased reading and math achievement, improved attendance, fewer behavioral problems, increased graduation rates, greater likelihood of employment and living independently after graduation, and social and emotional benefits. A 2016 meta-analysis of 280 studies from twenty-five countries found, "There is clear and consistent evidence that inclusive educational settings can confer substantial short and long-term benefits for students with and without disabilities."

Importantly, inclusive classrooms also have benefits for students without disabilities. Students without disabilities show reduced prejudice and fear of difference, and increased self-esteem and sense of belonging when they are educated alongside peers with disabilities. The academic effects of being educated in an inclusive environment are by large positive for students without disabilities. Thus, delaying the implementation of these regulations could also harm students without disabilities by depriving them the opportunity to interact with peers with disabilities that would be afforded by increased placement of students with disabilities in inclusive settings.

Nearly 70 years after Brown v. Board of Education, many K-12 schools remain racially segregated and unequal. What's dangerous about segregation is not just the racial separation, which social science research shows has very negative effects not just for students of color, but for white students who attend racially isolated schools. It's that the schools predominantly attended by students of color and students from low-income families also tend to be under-resourced.

These schools tend to lack resources like qualified and experienced teachers and school administrators. Segregation also contributes to school discipline disparities largely because many educators in under resourced schools are inexperienced and teaching in overcrowded low-quality facilities. All of these things profoundly impact students' experiences and outcomes in life.

The Media Trap

Ch. 2

The Media has incredible influence in shaping our political and cultural narratives. Often the most important message of a story is not explicitly stated. For instance, the media often report heavily on low level street crime like shoplifting while ignoring widespread corporate crime like wage theft, which has cost workers billions. The media is one of the main causes of collective paralysis.

Democracy requires informed individuals to function. In today's divided, profit-hungry media landscape, it's impossible to discern what is true and what's not. The media isn't holding up its vital function as the "fourth estate." The "Fourth Estate" refers to the news media, especially with regards to their role in the political process. The news media is often seen as a critical check on the power of the other three estates, serving as a watchdog to hold elected officials and other public figures accountable for their actions.

The press plays a crucial role in providing citizens with access to information about what is happening in government, as well as shining a light on corruption, abuse of power, and other forms of wrongdoing. In recent years, the role of the Fourth Estate has come under scrutiny, as the rise of social media and other digital platforms has challenged the traditional business model of the news media.

The rise of terms like *"fake news"* or "gotcha journalism" are symptoms of the failure of mass media to accurately present what is happening in the world. We can't make progress if we don't know what's indeed going on.

"When I grabbed him, the only way I can describe it is I felt like a five-year old holding onto Hulk Hogan," this was Ferguson's Officer Darren Wilson statement describing his altercation with unarmed black teenager Michael Brown.

Over the last half century Black Americans have made strides somewhat towards equality in America. The 44th president of the United States was a Black man. The 46th vice president of the United States is a Black female and yet Blacks still have significant barriers that linger. There is still very much inequity in education, employment, wealth, and within the criminal justice system.

Research and experience have shown that expectations and biases on the part of potential employers, teachers, and police officers, influence the life outcomes of Black males.

In the media, the caricatures and critiques of Black males usually pivot around negative stereotypes. The media systemically and inaccurately portray Black males as poor criminals from unstable communities. Black fathers are portrayed as absent deadbeats without any supporting evidence. People from all walks of life form their opinions about the Black community and specifically Black males from the media's duplicitous portrayals. Conversely, the positive images we see linked with black males in the media tend to be associated to a small, stereotypic set such as sports, and rap. I want you to really think about the last time you saw a black college professor, doctor, lawyer or scientist selling a product?

"Schools often treat Black families as if they have nothing to offer their own children. Their cultural wealth and knowledge are not addressed; it is not seen as an asset. Over and over again, I read research where Black parents share their perspectives of feeling marginalized, ridiculed, talked down to, and mistreated by school systems; yet these same parents are supposed to believe that when special education is presented to them, it is a solution to their child's difficulties?"

Aubry Threlkeld, Endicott College

As a Black male who grow up without a father and a mother who was addicted to drugs. I possess a wide range of complex insights and emotions. To be honest, Black males are a reservoir of information some constructive and some not so constructive. Image a young Black male whose hair is twisted (dreadlocks), his pants are sagging, his baseball cap backwards and his teeth are gold. This young man could very much be gifted. He could be an architect, a video game developer, or maybe even a teacher or engineer.

Unfortunately, he will be judged because of his "swag" (slang word that refers to stylish confidence). People might deem him to be something that he very well may not even be. Also, why is it that whenever the news covers low income schools and/or their parents it seems to be in a negative light. By portraying this narrative in the media, it will fundamentally match some people's negative bias that bad schools are synonymous with Black and Brown schools.

Many of us have brought into the negative stereotypes that's fed to us by the media. Not only have we brought into the stereotypes but for many of us they have become entrenched in our convictions as reality. Now that young Black male walking behind you at the mall, sitting across from you at the movies, or even walking into your classroom are seen as threats. Then the narrative shifts from educating his mind and inspiring his soul to control and policing of his body.

As Americas murky history has showed us, the prejudice against young Black males is no secret. Case in point, in 1989 Central Park jogger case, where five Black and Latino teenage boys were wrongfully convicted for the rape and beating of a young white woman in New York City. The young men age ranged between 13 and 16 years old, their images and likeness were slandered across the news; their names and addresses were released to the public. In retrospect this tragedy is a painful metaphor for society's angst and hostility toward young men of color. So many are unjustly presumed guilty before proven innocent. So many of our young Black and Brown men remain misunderstood, and seemingly invisible.

National public opinion data cited in a report from the University of Chicago's Black Youth Project reveals that Black youth "report the highest rate of harassment by the police," while fewer Black and Latino teens trust police or feel like "full and equal citizens" compared to peers of other racial groups. To add injury to insult, the murders of Eric Garner, Michael Brown, and George Floyd, among countless others, serve as grim reminders to young, disadvantaged men of color that their lives are devalued by so many in this country.

The increasing impact of these tragedies on Black males is what some intellectuals call a "speaking wound." These killings re-trigger in young Black men traumatic memories of racially charged encounters with strangers and police. This far-reaching form of stereotyping and oppression is called the "white gaze." The white gaze is a term popularized by critically acclaimed writer Toni Morrison. When describing how it operates, Morrison said that it's the idea that "Black lives have no meaning and no depth without the white gaze." In the simplest terms, the white gaze can be conceptualized as the assumed white reader.

During the school year of 2012, a white female student was hauled into the dean's office at Chicago's Hinsdale South High School for smoking weed. She confessed to getting high and told the police that three other students had been smoking weed with her. Three of the four students received punishment from the school. The girl and her friend who was also white, were suspended for five days. A male student who was white, received no punishment. However, the fourth student, a Black male, was not only suspended for a full week; he was also arrested and pleaded guilty to being in possession of drug paraphernalia.

Major media outlets routinely present a distorted picture of Black families portraying them as dependent and dysfunctional while white families are more likely to be depicted as sources of social stability, according to the report released by Color of Change, a racial justice organization, and Family Story, an advocate of diverse family arrangements.

"This leaves people with the opinion that Black people are plagued with self-imposed dysfunction that creates family instability and therefore, all their problems,"

Travis L. Dixon University of Illinois

The 46th President of the United States Joe Biden said, 'Poor Kids' are just as bright as 'White Kids.' President Biden was speaking in Des Moines, IA at an event hosted by the Asian & Latino Coalition. President Biden said that "We should challenge students in these schools," President Biden said. "We have this notion that somehow if you're poor, you cannot do it. Poor kids are just as bright and just as talented as white kids." He paused, then added: "Wealthy kids, black kids, Asian kids no I really mean it, but think how we think about it." Black kids are still perceived as academically inferior and are still labeled as defiant, destructive and hyperactive. I would imagine that some would think of America as being a pillar of equality especially for being known as the land of the free.

However, we all continue to witness the same calamity day in and day out within the walls of our classrooms and behind the gates of American prisons. Black males being treated unfairly. Black males being racial profiled. Black males being the victims of unconscious bias. This crisis originates in their homes, stretches into classrooms, and shoots them straight into the pipeline at extremely high numbers.

Decreasing incarceration rates for Black males might be a matter of improving educational outcomes for them. In his piece "A Broken Windows Approach to Education Reform," Forbes writer James Marshall Crotty makes a direct connection between drop-out and crime rates. He argues that if educators will simply take a highly organized approach to keeping kids in school, it will make a difference in the crime statistics of the future. However, that might be easier said than done!

Given the powerful influence that media can have on society, it is essential to you develop media literacy skills. Media literacy involves the ability to analyze and evaluate media messages critically. This includes understanding the persuasive techniques used in advertising, recognizing bias in news media, and evaluating the accuracy of information presented in various forms. Media literacy skills can help you make informed decisions about their media consumption and help you resist negative influences or "fake news". It can also empower you to create media messages that promote positive social norms and values.

Trapped in Soft Bigotry

Ch. 3

"Now some say it is unfair to hold disadvantaged children to rigorous standards," Bush remarked. "I say it is discrimination to require anything less, the soft bigotry of low expectations." A decade after Bush first utterer these words, not much has really changed in regards to educating Black males. All humans have traits of bias, if you think you're not bias then you are indeed bias to your bias.

If anyone has ever doubted that Black children especially Black males are not treated equally in the classroom they obviously have never looked at any research. When discussing inequality in the classroom, it's tempting to focus on external factors like socioeconomic status but it's taboo to address issues like teacher bias. After all, what teacher wants to on up to bias especially towards poor, helpless, and broken students. However, even the most enthusiastic, seasoned, and well-meaning teacher has stereotypes and beliefs that affect the way he or she teaches and interacts with his or her students.

I know that we all want to believe that teachers are superhuman, but they aren't. Teachers are very much human and influenced by psychological biases. This bias is when teachers assume that students behave in a way because of their character rather than in response to their environmental circumstances.

In education bias is directly associated with racial disparities in student achievement and discipline.

Unconscious bias is particularly relevant to Americans because we have such a wide achievement gap in education. When teachers form expectations (usually low) of their students based on reasons such as their gender, race, socioeconomic status, or information gained from another source it affects not just that one student-teacher relationship but the student's entire self-concept as well as more tangible measures like their GPA.

Addressing unconscious bias is imperative to improving educational outcomes, particularly for low-income students and minorities. Let's be honest, students who attend high poverty schools usually have:

Fewer Resources and Opportunities

High poverty schools have less experienced teachers, lower teacher salaries, are less likely to have critical math, science, and advanced coursework, spend less per student on instructors and instructional materials with state and local dollars, and have fewer advanced courses. All of this shows that students in high poverty schools many of whom have fewer resources and supports outside of the school building are also getting less in the classroom. And, it's largely students of color that are feeling these impacts.

Teacher Experience

Years of research has documented the challenges schools with concentrated poverty face in attracting and recruiting teachers and helping students succeed in the classroom. The unfortunate result is less experienced teachers in the classrooms of students with the greatest needs.

Instructional Spending

Teachers in high poverty schools also earn lower average salaries compared to low poverty schools, likely in part because of this discrepancy in teacher experience. The average teacher salary in high poverty schools was about $46,000 school year compared to over $57,000 in low poverty schools. Overall, there is lower instructional spending from the state and localities per student in high poverty schools than low poverty schools. High poverty schools spent 10 percent less per student on instructors (teachers and aides), instructional materials, and professional development than low poverty schools using state and local resources. That means schools are investing less on instruction in schools with students that start out with less and have greater needs outside of the classroom. High poverty schools with high percentages of students of color had even lower per student spending on instruction.

Course Offerings

High poverty middle schools and high schools are also less likely to offer advanced coursework compared to schools with low concentrations of poverty.

Worse Outcomes in High Poverty Schools

There are clear consequences to providing fewer resources to students in high poverty schools. Students in high poverty schools do worse on standardized tests, are more likely to be chronically absent during the school year, more likely to be held back in their grade, and less likely to graduate on-time.

Soft bigotry is when an educator doesn't expect certain students to meet the same standards of achievement as other students. It's called "soft bigotry" because it is a more subtle and subconscious form of prejudice. It irks my soul when I hear an educator say *"I don't see color with my students."* I have heard this statement more times than I can care to count and quite frankly, it offends me.

I believe their logic is somewhat pure and they really want me to be impressed with their color-blindness philosophy, but I'm not. When someone states that they do not see color, they are telling me that they are ignoring important specific details that comprise the character and being of that individual student. Each child comes into your classroom with different experiences, needs, thoughts, and perspectives.

That students skin color has a lot to do with their experiences, needs, thoughts, and perspectives. A recent study conducted by the university of Yale revealed that biases are directed at much younger children than what was previously thought.
Researchers led by Yale professor Walter Gilliam showed 135 educator's videos of children in a classroom setting.

Each video had a black boy and girl, and a white boy and girl. The teachers were told the following:

We are interested in learning about how teachers detect challenging behavior in the classroom. Sometimes this involves seeing behavior before it becomes problematic. The video segments you are about to view are of preschoolers engaging in various activities. Some clips may or may not contain challenging behaviors.

Your job is to press the enter key on the external keypad every time you see a behavior that could become a potential challenge. While the teachers were asked to detect "challenging behavior", no such behavior existed in any of the videos. Yet when asked which children required the most attention, 42% of the teachers identified the black boy.

The participants' conscious appraisal of whom they believed required the most attention closely mirrored the independent results of an eye-tracking technology used by the research team, which noted that preschool teachers "show a tendency to more closely observe black students, and especially males, when challenging behaviors are expected".

Black males are policed differently in the streets and in the classroom. Research demonstrates that Black males are viewed as years older than they actually are. Research also demonstrates that racial disparities in school discipline exist for Black students in the most subjective categories *"willful defiance"*, *"insubordination"*, *"disrespect"*.

Those racial disparities decrease significantly for the most objective of categories: possession of alcohol on campus, possession of drugs with intent to distribute, possession of a loaded weapon. Staff tend to observe more closely Black males when challenging behaviors are expected.

Jawanza Kunjufu, author of Black Students, Middle Class Teachers, wrote: "The most important factor impacting the academic achievement of African American children is not the race or gender of the teacher but the teacher's expectations." What you believe as an educator and how you perceive Black male students has a fundamental impact on how successful they will be in the classroom.

I am reminded of an incident where a white teacher asked all the black students (he didn't ask any white kids) that came through his classroom door of his honors class to show him their schedule as proof that they were in the right place. The teacher obviously assumed that the Black students were in the wrong room, I would imagine this gesture made the students feel unwelcome and/or humiliated.

One way to address bias that exist in the classroom could be to create anonymity in the grading process. In some ways, this is easier said than done. Teachers could ask their students to write their names on the back of their papers rather than at the top or have students turn their papers in electronically with student ID numbers rather than names. However, these methods involve complete student compliance, which is difficult to achieve and may add time to the grading process, which already overburdens most teachers.

"My first-year teaching, I was the BAC teacher at the middle school level. The BAC classroom was for those students that were self-contained because of behavioral issues in which they were classified as special education. The group I had ranged from 7-16 students throughout the school year. My immediate supervisor was the campus special education coordinator. We did not have one conversation the entire year about academics. She constantly wanted me to reward the students with toys and clothes, which were purchased with department or/and school funds that were approved. She also wanted me to pitch in to purchase a bike for the students to compete for at the end of the year, based on points earned as an incentive for good behavior. She essentially conveyed to me that she did not want me to focus on academics, that we needed to focus on rewards to incentivize behavior."

Mills Carnell Rodgers

Take me for instance; I have very defining characteristics that make me the man I am. One of which is that I am

Black, I am also a male, and a father and husband, just to name a few. However, being a Black male is probably the most important identity because it is the one characteristic that I am judged by every single time I leave my front door. When I walk into a room for a professional development people see a Black man first before they see a professional speaker.

If I am being prejudged day to day by the color of my skin, how can you as my teacher ignore it? When you teach, you must realize that the students coming into your classroom most likely have not had the same experiences that you may have had. Judging those students by your experiences tends to lead to institutional racism, so I ask you, how can you not see color?

On average about 13 percent of the student body in public schools are identified as SPED. Look at the totally number of Black male students in your school who are identified as SPED, then compare that to the demographics of your school. If the number of Black male students being identified is high, it's past time to have a conversation about changing that narrative.

Schools that are experiencing the most success are those that combine equity with quality. These schools put their students in position for long term success. Equity is not the only solution for Black males but it is one of the most needed solutions for Black males in public schools, especially since Black male students are the population that many educators struggle to connect with the most.

Equity allows Black males to have access to highly enriched educational resources they need to be successful. It's refreshing to see the conversation about Black males and equity growing. Black males are often denied access to key resources because of bias, stereotypes about their academic performance, character, and ability. Education is building for a better life. It's not simply passing a test to build up your academic data. You have to seriously consider what equity looks like in your school for Black males when they still rank highest in student dropout rates and lowest in literacy rates.

Public schools need to have stronger methods of implementation and accountability. Black males need strong advocates at the White House willing to invest money so that the programs providing equitable services are readily available when needed. It's important to ask the right questions not only when at the table but across the board.

Let's be honest public schools cannot have strong turnaround plans without having Black males at the forefront. Although the conversation on Black males and equity is growing, unfortunately, there are those in public education who are still battling what W.E.B DuBois said, *"Education must not simply teach work; it must teach life!"* Equity begins with improving the educational experience for Black males in public schools as well as the teachers and parents supporting them. No child Black, Brown, or White in America should be *segregated by low expectations, imprisoned by illiteracy,* abandoned to frustration and the darkness of self-doubt.

Understanding the Brain: Unconscious or implicit biases are social stereotypes about people that we form without our conscious awareness. They are essentially mental "shortcuts" that allow us to make fast decisions under pressure. We all have them, and they are triggered automatically and outside of our control when we feel strong emotions like stress or fear. If we perceive a threat, a small but very influential part of our brains called the amygdala, or limbic system, triggers a fight, flight or freeze response before we have a chance to process whether the threat is real or not. The good news is that we are more than our amygdala.

Our brains are primarily made up of what's called the neocortex, which helps us reason and manage our responses. That means we can train ourselves to take a moment to process what's happening and determine what our course of action should be in a way that goes beyond our first impulse. Knowing how the brain works is critical to understanding how race operates. Most of our actions occur without our conscious awareness.

The amygdala, hippocampus, and prefrontal cortex make up the control panel for bias. The brain relies on shortcuts all the time. We use what we've learned from our environment to make quick assumptions about whom to trust, how to behave, what to say. But shortcuts can sometimes lead us astray. *You can't always trust your brain.*

According to Dr. Mahzarin R. Banaji, *mind-bugs* are engrained patterns of thought that lead to errors in how we perceive, remember, reason, and make decisions. What about my brain? Is there bias there too? The amygdala fires up for our fears, the hippocampus records our memories, and the prefrontal cortex controls our ability to reason and reconsider. Bias is in our brains from early in childhood. But having bias does not mean that we are destined to be bad people. Those same brain processes can sometimes be used for good.

Bias in all its forms based upon race, gender, sexual orientation, religion, politics or any other group affiliation is more readily seen as a deliberate choice than as an unintentional predisposition. Nevertheless, research indicates that human beings innately perceive anyone that is different from them as a threat because their brain has an evolutionary requirement to do so.

"The capacity to discern 'us' from 'them' is fundamental in the human brain," wrote David Amodio, associate professor of psychology and neural science at New York University, in his 2014 paper, "The neuroscience of prejudice and stereotyping." "Although this computation takes just a fraction of a second, it sets the stage for social categorization, stereotypes, prejudices, intergroup conflict and inequality," he wrote.

Through socialization, our brains have created visual and aural categories for most of the sights we see and sounds we hear. This process is referred to as 'implicit social cognition." Humans use categories for people as well as objects. Based upon visual and aural cues, we make automatic judgments about what category a particular person fits within and we often act on those judgments.

These categories and judgments normally serve us well. However, we can obviously be wrong. Our errors are usually meaningless not recognizing that a small flat object playing a song is an mp3 player and not a cell phone. In some instances, these errors can be life-threatening the object in a man's hand is a cell phone and not a gun. Why might the life-threatening errors occur more in some situations than others? Because categories also influence what people pay attention to, how they organize their attention, and what they later remember (Whitley & Kite, 2010; Hamilton, 1981).

Not surprisingly, our brain's automatic use of categories is particularly risky with respect to humans. Categorization can activate stereotypes that hamper rather than help our assessment of how to behave or respond in a given situation (e.g. Hamilton & Sherman, 1994). The widespread stereotype of Black criminality makes it more likely that a cell phone will appear to be gun if the man holding it is Black rather than White.

Scientists define stereotypes as the beliefs and opinions people hold about the characteristics, traits, and behaviors of a certain group (Allport, 1954; Macrae, Mile, Bodenhausen, 1994; Hilton & Von Hippel, 1996). Stereotypes often cause us to make assumptions (both negative and positive) about people based upon superficial characteristics (Schneider, 2004). Media plays a significant role in shaping our perceptions of race.

For many Whites and people of other races and ethnicities, the media's portrayal of Black males is the primary basis for their knowledge and emotional reaction. With a few notable examples in politics, most media present Black males as figures to be admired for their athleticism, artistic or entertainment talent, or feared for their criminality.

While the vast majority of educators unquestionably have the best of intentions, the evidence is strong that implicit bias is affecting the 21st century student. National statistics on school suspension paint a particularly grim portrait of the fate of Black males. A male student of color who is suspended is three times as likely to drop out of school by the 10th grade and is in turn three times as likely to end up incarcerated (Goertz, Pollack, & Rock, 1996).

One little-known but chilling marker of this disproportionality is that, by the age of 15, roughly 2% of the Black male American population is simply missing; these boys are neither in school nor in the criminal justice system. They are most likely alive, but they are utterly disenfranchised from society (Flynn, 2008). This is a fate suffered by no other demographic group in America.

Eliminating Implicit Bias: The first step is to be real with yourself. Very few educators will openly admit to harboring bigoted beliefs or unconscious biases that would affect their day to day decision-making. But the truth is that we all have biases. *"The first step is awareness,"* says German Gomez, assistant general counsel of Hogan Lovells U.S. LLP. I think all of us in the educational profession need to remind ourselves that there's potentially something lurking in our brains that could cause us to make decisions that aren't thought through or subjective.

Recognize that bias is all around you. Unconscious bias does not exist in a vacuum. Unconscious or implicit bias is developed through a person's upbringing, peers and/or religion. The media also plays an immense role in contributing to bias. Karen Hester, CEO of the Center for Legal Inclusiveness, cites news coverage of Hurricane Katrina as an example.

An image of white people with food in the middle of the flooding bore a caption that referred to them as "finding" food from a grocery store, while a similar picture of a black man featured a caption that claimed he "looted" the food. Janie Schulman, a partner at Morrison & Foerster LLP in Los Angeles, suggests popular culture also influences implicit bias. She cites the movie, "Hidden Figures," as an example in which the white male NASA scientists assume Katherine Johnson is a secretary because she is black, but she is actually a physicist.

The Thomas Meyer study, a legal writing analysis, demonstrates implicit racial bias in the legal profession. Conducted in 2014, the study included 60 partners from 22 firms of various sizes. The diverse group of partners were tasked with reviewing a memo written by a third-year associate by the name of Thomas Meyer: half of the partners were told Thomas Meyer was a white man and half were told he was black.

The white Thomas Meyer received a 4.1/5 score on his memo, while the black Thomas Meyer received a 3.2/5. The memos had the same amount of spelling errors, yet the group analyzing the black Meyers paper found more spelling errors than the group with the white Meyers paper.

Take measures to challenge and/or eliminate your biases. Eliminating bias is only possible if educators are able to recognize and understand their own biases. Implicit association tests, which can be found online, can help educators understand if they have certain biases outside of their own awareness. Once you realize your own biases, you can actively challenge them.

Ways to Eliminate Implicit Bias in Your Teaching Instruction
Avoid Fixed Mindset. Carol Dweck did research on fixed mindset vs. the growth mindset. With a fixed mindset, you believe there's

nothing to learn and no way to grow. With a growth mindset, you see yourself as a work in progress. It is the job of educators to foster a growth mindset of all their students regardless of gender, race, or ethnicity. With a growth mindset, there is more brain activity and all students can grow.

As an educator, take the time and acknowledge holidays of all cultures of those students who you are teaching. Provide an environment where students feel comfortable, valued, and appreciated. Provide equitable practices for all students regardless of race, ethnicity, gender, sexuality, special education students etc. Work to increase empathy and empathic communication. Get real and embrace discomfort. Spend time with people who are not like yourself.

If bias continues to exist in classrooms it could actually widen the achievement gap for students. As educators, we should look at students as individuals and provide equitable quality instruction daily that will increase student achievement. When we create a culture of inclusion, it creates an environment that is conducive for teaching and learning. Students feel valued, respected, and appreciated which leads to increased motivation, confidence, and achievement.

When we need to make immediate, life-saving decisions, unconscious biases are often a good thing. However, in our day-to-day lives, they can blind us from receiving relevant, valuable information that, in the long run, will benefit us. Taking a moment to be mindful of our biases and their effect on others is a positive step in the right direction.

And finally, Stop Coddling Black Males!

They already feel entitled to the things it took their parents 30 years to obtain. So many of them have never had to earn anything but virtually have everything with horrible grades, bad attitudes, and disrespectful ways. If children are not given responsibilities and work at a young age, it's harder to instill the ethic when they're older. You're doing your Black male students a great disservice if you just baby them and give them unmerited grades.

By encouraging your students to work for what they get, you'll be teaching them valuable skills that they will carry with them the rest of their life. During the early 1900s kids were working 60 hours a week in factories and coal mines. While it was a deplorable situation, it shows that kids are capable of taking on far greater tasks than parents today are willing to give them.

We have to absolutely stop coddling and enabling Black males. It's a problem that's going to spread through our society like wildfire. It's not fair to society, and more importantly, is not fair to Black males to teach them this is okay. It will not serve them well towards a successful and happy life. There's a big difference between supporting kids who are having trouble and enabling them.

The best teachers of life are usually low-stakes mistakes. Bubble-wrapping Black males can only mean one thing a weakened mental immune system where even the slightest changes to the environment around them are enough to throw them off their game. *"Prepare your students for the road, not the road for your*

Students: Jonathan Haidt and Greg Lukianoff, The coddling of the American Mind.

Stress Trap

Ch. 4

The teaching field is one of the more burned out career fields nationally, but the pandemic exacerbated existing challenges and introduced new ones to a profession already struggling. The return to the classroom hasn't meant a return to normality (whatever that is) for many teachers. Students are struggling to recover both academically and emotionally from the pandemic. Continued teacher shortages are adding even more to an already full plate. Not to mention, teachers still run the risk of contracting covid19.

Teachers who are burned out are commonly more irritable, less hopeful, they feel helpless, incompetent, emotionally exhausted, isolated and very cynical towards their students and their work. When you're an educator, it's easy to convince yourself that you're okay and you should just push through those overwhelming feelings. After all, as an educator you have a ton of students relying on you with a plethora of problems to solve, and many educators feel like they don't have the time nor space to take a step back and deal with their mounting stress and exhaustion.

Unfortunately for human's burnout is not just something that disappears overnight. The brains of teachers who are chronically burnt-out show similar damage as people who have experienced extreme trauma.

"The mental health and well-being of teachers can have a really important impact on the mental health and well-being of the children who they're spending most of their days with, having teachers feel safe and supported in their school environments is essential to students learning and being successful."

Jennifer Greif Green Boston University

Lisa Sanetti, a professor of educational psychology at the University of Connecticut, says, "Chronically stressed teachers are just less effective in the classroom."

Recent studies report that educators stress levels rank right up there with other highly stressful professions such as nursing and law enforcement. This is leading to burnout and high levels of turnover, which creates both monetary and emotional costs for school districts and students. The teacher shortage in the U.S. is intensifying to say the least.

"This crisis has been coming for a long time. Forget about replacing them with someone of the same quality. I'm just worried about replacing them. Period."

David Pennington, superintendent

High poverty school districts are being hit the hardest. This is a recent study by the Gallup Panel Workforce Study, conducted in February of 2022, with 12,319 U.S. full-time employees, including 1,263 K-12 workers. Within the K-12 employee population, teachers are the most burned out, at 52%.

"The reality is, when you're living it, you're just trying to get to the end of the day successfully and try again tomorrow,"

Unknow Educator

Teaching can be a very rewarding profession however, it can also be very toxic to your health. Without the proper support, teachers are in danger of being overworked which can lead to mismanaging one's own mental and physical health needs. Ever heard the popular saying "health is wealth"? This gives large meaning to one's life, as health is considered the most valuable and precious thing humans process. Good health means not only the absence of disease in the body but a complete physical, mental, social as well as spiritual well-being of an individual. It has always been ridiculous for me to hear someone say to a room full of educators, "you should never take your work home with you." the truth is, it's hard to be an effective educator and not.

Burnout is a state of emotional, physical, and mental exhaustion caused by excessive and prolonged stress. It occurs when you feel overwhelmed, emotionally drained, and unable to meet the constant demands of education. As the stress continues, one begins to lose interest and motivation that led them to take on a certain role in the first place. The negative effects of burnout spills over into every area of one's life including home, work, and social life.

Burnout is a gradual process. It doesn't happen overnight, but it can creep up on you. The signs and symptoms are subtle at first, but become worse as time goes on. While burnout isn't a diagnosable psychological disorder, that doesn't mean it shouldn't be taken seriously.

Eventually, you may feel like you have nothing more to give. Burnout can also cause long-term changes to your body that make you vulnerable to illnesses like colds and flu. Because of its many consequences, it's important to deal with burnout right away. Let's keep it real, we all know an educator who has "had enough." An educator who constantly complains to anyone that will listen.

Who is exhausted by the ratio of classroom discipline to actual teaching. This state of education in America is bad not only for educators, but for students as well especially Black males in SPED. If we want to solve these issues, if we want to produce happier students and teachers, it's time to take a hard look at the many questions surrounding teacher burnout: it's definitions, causes, symptoms, prevention and more.

I empathize with the issues many teachers have to face in the 21st century. Classrooms are overcrowded and often they are trying to teach a range of children with varying cognitive abilities, behavioral issues, and considerably varied environmental circumstances. It certainly isn't what teaching was 30 years ago.

Teachers have to juggle issues involving weapons, drugs, and sexual harassment all while remaining politically correct and nurturing.

Whether facing an unrealistic parent or a traumatized student, teachers are expected to do it all with a smile on their face. Sure, teachers have aides that can help out in some circumstances but being asked to multi-task constantly with eyes and ears behind your head all the while being expected to deliver top-notch instruction to each child at his/her particular level is a bit like asking a Black cardiovascular surgeon to perform a heart transplant while simultaneously giving a Black Lives Matter speech to the KKK.

Let's face it multi-tasking at any job can cause people to often feel nothing really gets done, because in reality, sometimes nothing does. Teachers often feel they are caught in a cycle of constantly being asked to do more with less. Those I encounter who are employed in the educational setting, often tell me they simply feel "out of control". Everyone from administrators and parents to society tells them how to do their job.

Although, that might be the case for other professions as well, I think feeling "out of control" is particularly disheartening for teachers. Teachers hold the future in their hands and when they feel unable to do what they were trained to do, that future looks bleak for the students as well as for the educators.

Asking for help isn't a crime! if those around you aren't aware that you're feeling the way you feel, they can't help you. It's a leader's job to manage their team and ensure they can cope with the workload. Asking for help isn't a sign of weakness, it's a sign of strength. Accept that a "to do list" or "lesson plans" rarely gets completed during the day to day activities of an educator.

Especially in a title one school. Focus on what you can control. It may sound cliché, but if you're going to teach and remain sane, you have to learn to let some things go. Learn to choose your battles with students, other teachers, parents, and even some administrators. While you may play an important role in your students' lives inside your classroom, there are aspects related to their home lives that you will never be able to control.

Learn to say no. Humans often find difficultly uttering the word no to others, especially to those they care about. Saying no requires an inner self awareness and power that very few have. Some people say yes just to avoid conflicts, and/or confrontations. If you find it challenging to say no try saying something such as, "I'll have to check my calendar first, can I get back to you?"

Then if you find it hard to say no face to face, send them a text or email messages instead. But in order to safeguard your sanity in education you have to learn how to say no. Stop with the pity parties and feeling guilty also. As well as learning to say no it's also important to let go of guilt. It isn't easy guilt is a tough emotion to deal with.

Stop taking everything so personally and learn to manage your expectations. It's important that your desire for excellence, growth and greatness doesn't make you become too idealistic. Honestly, it is important to remember that we work with real people; people who make mistakes despite best efforts and who don't operate perfectly all of the time. Everyone has a bad day. Everyone hurts. Everyone has weaknesses. Extend grace, my friend, because you'd desire the same. Bad leadership burn teachers out as well. In schools there are bullies, many egos and the occasional school leaders who are just not up to doing the job required. Thankfully it is rare, but it does exist. The chances are, they are probably not reading this book.

It seems that every article, social media post and book these days is about teacher burnout, issues with the current educational system, or lack of parental or administrative support for teachers. While many of these articles speak to the true challenges' teachers face every day, what gets lost or muted is that the vast majority of teachers find great satisfaction in their work.

Despite the everyday challenges' teachers face, a number of surveys conducted among teachers indicate that the vast majority of them are satisfied with their job. For example, the School and Staffing Survey by the National Center for Education Statistics, found that nine out of 10 teachers responded with "satisfied" or "very satisfied" when asked about their teaching career. Also, a survey of America's Best Teachers found that most teachers feel and appreciate recognition they receive from colleagues, students and parents of students.

Teaching is one of the most fulfilling professions in the world. There a number of reasons why teachers love this profession. One of the most valued aspects of teaching is the ability to take a broken student and help him or her see their greatness. Teachers typically report the daily "aha" moments as the most rewarding aspect of their job. Seeing students finally make a breakthrough and understand something they've been struggling with allows teachers to feel the direct impact of their work on a daily basis.

A career in teaching is one of the most recession-proof careers according to CNBC News. This is because even in times such as the Covid19 pandemic communities still needed teachers. Jobs closed people went home but teachers were still teaching virtually from their homes. The field of education is expected to see a steady increase, on par with the national average, with 1.9 million new job openings between 2014 and 2024, according to the U.S. Bureau of Labor Statistics (BLS). Teaching is full of little joys you simply can't quantify. Jenna Wiley, in her Huffington Post blog titled 11 Reasons Teaching is the Best (Even When It Isn't), teacher talks about the simple, silly, every-day joys of teaching.

For example, the joys of student birthdays, school pajama days, and my favorite building those relationships with hard to reach kids and discovering that they are really great kids. Then there are the funny things kids say without intending to be funny, their genuineness, and their sense of curiosity. These and so such more are what energizes school days and makes teachers excited about going to work.

The bottom line is that while teaching can be a tough and demanding job, for those who are looking to make a difference in the world, it can be one of the most rewarding and satisfying professions. Districts are trying to help with yoga classes, counseling sessions and webinars on mental health. Some teachers have organized trivia nights or online happy hours where colleagues can just vent. Teachers told NPR they force themselves to take breaks, go for a bike ride or call a friend. Some have started therapy.

How to Help Reduce Teacher Stress
Positive Behavior Supports

When teachers have improved student behavior in the classroom, increased sense of self-efficacy, and reduced anxiety and stress, there will be a corresponding decrease in teacher attrition and burnout. According to Thibodeaux, et al. (2015), student discipline is a top reason for teachers leaving the classroom. Student discipline needs to be more actively considered among the important variables to address teacher attrition (Ramos, J. & Hughes, T., 2020.)

There is a growing body of research that supports improvements in disciplinary behavior, anti-social behavior, student bullying behavior, and peer victimization. These are directly related to implementing systematic positive behavior support systems, also known as PBIS (Bradshaw, Koth, Thornton, & Leaf, 2009). Schools delivering PBIS methods with fidelity displayed lower levels of disruptive behavior problems and more prosocial behavior.

There were also significant reductions in office discipline referrals (Bradshaw, C., Waasdorp, T., Leaf, P., 2012). Therefore, district and school leaders should strongly consider implementing the tenets of PBIS across all classrooms, which will improve teacher working conditions and school climate, thus increasing teacher retention and reducing the incidence of professional burnout.

A child with challenging behavior who has an Individualized Education Program (IEP), should have positive behavioral interventions included to help reduce challenging behaviors and support the new behavioral skills to be learned through the IEP goals. These interventions should be specific strategies that are positive and proactive, and are not reactive and consequence-based. The following list suggests some different kinds of positive behavioral interventions that could be useful:

Clear routines and expectations that are posted and reviewed help children know what comes next in their school day, reducing anxiety or fear. Stop, Relax, and Think strategy teaches children how to think about a problem and find a solution. After children understand the steps, role-play and practice can help the process become habit.

Helping children to recognize their own response to stress (clenched hands, voice tone, etc.) may become part of the instruction needed to use this strategy effectively. Practicing and being successful with these steps can take time for children. Therefore, it is important to consider what kind of support a child may need that will help reinforce progress.

Pre-arranged signals can be used to let a child know when he or she is doing something that is not acceptable. A hand motion, a shake of the head or a colored card placed on a desk as the teacher moves through the room could alert the child without drawing attention to the child or the behavior. It is important to develop a signal that the child and teacher agree on using and for what purpose.

Proximity control means that a teacher or adult moves closer to the child in a gentle way. If the teacher does not get the child's attention by using cues, then he or she may move closer to the student or give the lesson while standing near the child's desk. Planned response method is useful in stopping non-serious behaviors that are bothersome to other children or adults nearby.

For example, students who interrupt the class to attract the teacher's attention usually are successful in getting the teachers to respond. Planned response method acknowledges that children's challenging behaviors serve a purpose. If the purpose of that behavior is to gain your attention, then not providing attention means that the behavior does not work.

The behavior lessens over time and eventually disappears. Ignoring non-serious behavior is especially useful for parents when their child is having a tantrum for attention. Many adults find it difficult to ignore behaviors, especially if the behaviors interrupt what the adult is doing. Also, attention-seeking behaviors often get worse before they eventually get better.

Planned response method is not appropriate for behaviors that are considered extremely disruptive. This method also may not work if other children laugh at the problem behaviors the adult is trying to ignore. Some behaviors, including those that are unsafe or that include peer issues such as arguing, can grow quickly into more serious behaviors. It may not be possible to ignore these kinds of behaviors. The process of ignoring the behavior should never be used for unsafe behaviors. As children grow older and want attention more from their friends than from adults, the planned response method is less useful.

Discipline privately. Many children see it as a challenge when teachers attempt to discipline them in front of their peers. Children rarely lose these challenges, even when adults use negative consequences. Young people can gain stature from peers by publicly refusing to obey the teacher. A child is more likely to accept discipline if his or her peers are not watching the process.

Find opportunities for the child to help others. For example, a child who is using negative behaviors as a way to get out of class could be given the task of running an errand for the teacher to the front office. Peer involvement is another motivator for appropriate behavior. Finding times for the child who uses disruptive behavior to get attention from his classmates to help another student positively engages attention and can build rapport.

Positive phrasing lets children know the positive results for using appropriate behaviors. As simple as it sounds, this can be difficult. Teachers and parents are used to focusing on misbehavior. Warning children about a negative response to problem behaviors often seems easier than describing the positive impact of positive behaviors.

Compare the difference between positive phrasing and negative phrasing:

Positive phrasing: "If you finish your reading by recess, we can all go outside together and play a game."

Negative phrasing: "If you do not finish your reading by recess, you will have to stay inside until it's done."

Tangible, token, and activity reinforcers are also effective ways to encourage and support appropriate behavior. Tangible reinforcers can be awards, edibles or objects. Token reinforcers are tokens or points given for appropriate behavior that can be exchanged for something of value. Activity reinforcers are probably the most effective and positive as they allow students to participate in preferred activities, usually with other students, which also builds in social reinforcement.

Instructional Coaching

The empirical evidence is convincing that instructional coaches reduce teacher attrition and improve teacher retention (Long, 2009). Presumably, instructional coaches can improve professional efficacy and personal accomplishment so teachers feel they are having positive impacts on their students. According to current research, instructional coaching positively impacts outcomes for teachers regarding burnout (Aguilar, 2018).

The converging evidence is that making instructional coaches available to teachers, through high-quality guidance and collaboration, has the potential to mitigate the teacher retention crisis (Russel, J., 2019) and the potential onset of professional burnout. Instructional coaching can also increase the degree and quality of administrative support provided to teachers. Hughes et al. (2015) found that there are several areas of administrative support that are critical for reducing stress for teachers:

Emotional support: Teachers report that emotional support (e.g., reasonable expectations, trust, supportive environment) is essential.

Environmental support: The second most important kind of support is defined as "environmental support," exhibited when administrators effectively address negative student behavior and safety issues.

Instructional support: The third most important kind of support is instructional support, where teachers receive quality professional growth/development opportunities along with adequate resources and have a say in decisions that affect them (Harris, S., Davies, R., Christensen, S., Hanks, J., & Bowles, B., 2019).

Enhanced Administrative Support: Administrative support for teachers is an important external factor for mitigating teacher burnout. A study of nearly 8,000 teachers (Kraft, Simon & Lyon, 2020) across nine states showed that leaders play a key role in supporting teachers' sense of success, particularly when the leaders focused on strong communication and collaboration with teachers. According to teachers, lack of administrator support is reported to be the most critical component of school working conditions and can result in a nearly doubling of the teacher attrition rate (Sutcher, et al., 2019).

Kraft and Papay (2014) found that teachers who work in more supportive environments tend to develop skills and attributes that enable them to become more effective in increasing student achievement over time compared to teachers who report working in less supportive schools. Teachers frequently report that school leaders do not provide adequate support and expertise in dealing with student discipline issues. To improve administrative support in this area, we must provide school leaders with the knowledge and skills to implement consistent school-wide discipline methods such as PBIS.

Smaller Classes: If a teacher has smaller class sizes it has been proven that students learn faster and perform better. A class size of fewer than 20 students often results in more individual attention, increased participation, and better communication between the instructor and students. Students not only receive more feedback from their peers and instructors, they also tend to encounter more opportunities for hands-on learning than those in large classes.

Teachers have more flexibility to use different instructional approaches. Teachers have more time to teach because there are fewer discipline problems. Students are more likely to participate in class and become more involved. Teachers have more time to cover additional material and use more supplementary texts and enrichment activities.

Increased Teacher Autonomy: Giving teachers more autonomy can improve job satisfaction, improve retention, and reduce burnout. Multiple studies highlight the mediating effect of teacher autonomy in determining the effectiveness of school systems and structures.

Teacher involvement in the design and implementation of learning opportunities is essential to effectively improve teacher morale and student achievement. Additionally, systems that minimize administrative paperwork and set clear expectations for students and families can relieve pressure on teachers and reduce burnout (Santoro, 2021).

Trauma-Informed Approach: Mental health problems have risen among children and adults alike since the pandemic began, and educators are often the first to confront the effects of anxiety in the classroom. The Los Angeles Unified schools even launched a professional development course for its principals on how to implement trauma-informed supports for their staff and students.

Sympathy Trap

Ch. 5

The terms empathy and sympathy are often thrown around but very few actually grasp there true meaning. The term empathy was first introduced in 1909 by psychologist Edward B. Titchener as a translation of the German term einfühlung (meaning "feeling into"). Education has to be more than just teaching students, it is about building connections that encompasses the student mind, body and soul.

If you could stand in your students' shoes for 24 hours and hear what they hear. See what they see. Feel what they feel. Would you view and or treat them differently?

It's almost impossible in the 21st century to read an article about education and it not stress the importance of equity or empathy. Empathy in regards to education is a concerned educator's reaction to a student's personal feelings. It involves thinking, feeling, and even a physical reaction from you as an educator. While sympathy and compassion are in the same family as empathy, there are some significant differences. Sympathy is simply telling someone how you feel about their situation and moving on with your day. Empathy is when you care about how the person views what has happened to them. Sympathy is often thought to be more of a passive action, while empathy generally involves a much more involved active approach to understand the other person's plight. Some people lack empathy and, therefore, aren't able to understand what another person may be experiencing or feeling. This can result in behaviors that seem uncaring or sometimes even hurtful.

Fortunately, humans can become more empathic. As humans we have to work on listening to people without interrupting them. Pay attention to their body language and other types of nonverbal communication they may exhibit. Try to understand others, even when you don't agree with their point of view. Ask questions, if you would like to know something and don't just assume. ***Assuming is the enemy to an effective classroom.*** Empathy and sympathy are two terms that are often used interchangeably. But only one of them allows educators and students to connect on a deeper level.

Understanding the unique differences between empathy and sympathy can help an educator choose the most appropriate one given the circumstances. While empathy supports a deeper connection, there are times when a sympathetic response maybe more appropriate. However, sympathy can something lead to you offering unsolicited advice. Be careful because it's very easy when being sympathetic to be judgmental. In most cases sympathy does the direct opposite and doesn't help educators build those deep connections with students that is very much needed.

This is because sympathy really only offers surface-level understanding. It doesn't allow you to see the situation from the student's perspective. On the other hand, empathy lets you walk in someone else's shoes. As a result, you can better provide what they really need.

Empathy plays an important role in human, social, and psychological interaction during all stages of a student's life. Emotions are the DNA of the human experience. Social relationships play a pivotal role in helping humans become fully human. Connectedness is a fundamental need for students. Empathy especially in education is often deemed a "soft skill." Sometimes we equate empathy with coddling of students. Which it is not. As educators, many of us begin the school year with good intentions.

Then, the academic rush starts. Lesson plans are due. Grades pile up. Parent conferences begin. Student behavior disrupts our lessons and strains our patience. IEP's and faculty meetings fill our calendars. Believe it or not, students watch teachers constantly, and our actions can unintentionally display unempathetic behavior.

An eye-roll after a fellow teacher makes a comment models a mindset that lacks empathy to our students. In doing this, teachers are tacitly demonstrating that these behaviors are acceptable. If teachers don't want students to make a face, roll their eyes, or respond sarcastically to a serious comment, then they must model how to respond differently when interacting with other adults.

While the concept of teaching an emotion might seem ancient, research has shown that emotion can and should be taught within the classroom. In fact, in most cases, empathy has to be taught; it isn't developed on its own, but requires someone to put in intentional effort to strengthen. Being empathetic requires us to have perception we must put ourselves in others' shoes, which can be difficult when their experiences are foreign to us.

In best case scenarios, empathy is what pushes us to stand up for others, particularly when it comes to injustice and inequality. The development of empathy is crucial in building 21st Century Skills, particularly critical thinking and leadership skills. Many teachers incorporate empathy in their class to a degree, maybe without even knowing it.

English teachers encourage critical thinking and empathy when they ask students to put themselves in the shoes of characters in a book they're reading. Social Studies teachers who ask students to imagine what it would be like to be alive during a historical time period are encouraging the growth of empathy through creativity and perspective taking. While activities like these encourage empathy, students won't see the connection between empathy and other beneficial skills unless educators make them clear.

When frustrated with students, pause and take a deep breath and try to see the situation from their perspective before responding. When a student is upset try to understand his behavior before redirecting the behavior. Be aware of students' non-verbal cues and follow up on them. For example, if a student is slumping in her chair and appearing withdrawn or angry, say something like "are you okay, you weren't your normal chattering self today?" rather than immediately saying "pick your head up or get out".

Ask for students' input when appropriate and feasible (for example, when establishing classroom rules or generating ideas for group projects) and really listen. Find opportunities to incorporate their feedback and respond to their needs. One the other hand, be very cautious of the traps associated with empathy.

The first is the "At Least" Trap. This comment is very toxic and initiatives the other person's disconnection. You say, "I'm sorry," which is a great start, but then you start comparing the other persons suffering to someone else's suffering. And the opportunity for empathy is lost. In this context, that response seems ridiculous, right? And it is.

But it's also a really common way to respond to other people's problems. It's irresistible to try and put a silver lining on it, with *but* or *at least*. I know I am guilty of it. My excuse is that I am "helping them" see the bright side. And while that certainly has a place, when people are being vulnerable about a problem, it's normally way more effective to just sit and listen.

Empathy vs Sympathy Quiz

1. "You poor thing" _____
   Sympathy or Empathy?

2. "I've been there, it sucks" _____
   Sympathy or Empathy?

3. "I'm so sorry for you" _____
   Sympathy or Empathy?

4. "That looks terrible" _____
   Sympathy or Empathy?

5. "I can't imagine how bad this is for you" _____
   Sympathy or Empathy?

6. "What I am hearing you say is....Is that how you are feeling?"
   Sympathy or Empathy?

7. "How did you get yourself into this mess?" _____
   Sympathy or Empathy?

8. "You know, it's not that bad" _____
   Sympathy or Empathy?

9. "I feel bad for you" _____
   Sympathy or Empathy?

10. "I know what it is like down here" _____
   Sympathy or Empathy?

11. "You are not alone" _____
   Sympathy or Empathy?

12. "I feel that way too sometimes" _____
   Sympathy or Empathy?

Empathy vs Sympathy Answer Key

1. "You poor thing" **Sympathy**

2. "I've been there, it sucks" **Empathy**

3. "I'm so sorry for you" **Sympathy**

4. "That looks terrible" **Sympathy**

5. "I can't imagine how bad this is for you" **Sympathy**

6. "What I am hearing you say is….Is that how you are feeling?" **Empathy**

7. "How did you get yourself into this mess?" **Sympathy**

8. "You know, it's not that bad" **Sympathy**

9. "I feel bad for you" **Sympathy**

10. "I know what it is like down here" **Empathy**

11. "You are not alone" **Empathy**

12. "I feel that way too sometimes" **Empathy?**

Trapped in Inequity

Ch. 6

Inequity is perhaps one of the most damning issues we face in education. It has multiple causes, and its consequences include differences in access to schooling, retention and, more importantly, learning. Although America has made great progress in both absolute and relative numbers of enrolled students, the differences between the richest and the poorest, as well as those living in rural and urban areas, has not diminished. There are many explanations for educational inequity. In my view, the most important ones are the following: Equity and equality are not the same thing. Equality means providing the same resources to everyone. Equity signifies giving more to those most in need.

As with all students in our schools, the social and emotional health of Black males has to be of the highest priority. We have to make sure we are constantly acknowledging them, building them up and listening to them. This is a great starting place for providing Black males with a culturally responsive education. Culturally responsive practices and strategies help support and promote Black males.

Black males' matter, and they need, want, and deserve nothing less. Let's approach this from a different perspective. As educators lets focus on what Black males know, understand, and can do as opposed to what they can't do or what they do not know and/or understand.

Culturally responsive teachers wouldn't engage Black males from a deficit perspective (i.e., having "problems to fix" or being "at risk"). Instead, they seek to learn about their strengths, gifts, and talents.

In education, we think that sustained periods of sitting quiet is great classroom management. However, long periods of sitting quiet can actually undermine a child's verve. The term *verve* is often used to describe vigor and spirit or enthusiasm; in education, it refers to having high levels of energy being physically active and loud when mentally stimulated. Verve is a great description of how many Black males behave when they are excited about learning.

Another common indicator of classroom readiness is how well students follows instructions. While following rules can help ensure school safety and establish expectations. Educators should be very cautious because these rules could stifle a child's expressive individualism. Black males, and other children, benefit from being creative and taking risks as they explore, experiment, and follow where their curiosity leads them. Knowing this, culturally responsive teachers are able to be flexible in the ways they interpret "good behavior."

Culturally responsive teachers should also consider the implicit bias of obeying instructions without challenging authority figures. This expectation of obedience clashes culturally with Black students. Blunt and direct communication is often perceived as rude and/or disrespectful. In contrast, a culturally responsive teacher has to acknowledge Black students' cultural heritages as legacies that affect dispositions and attitudes.

Many educators today are clearly not adequately prepared to educate Black males and these students are paying a severe price.

Whether by ignorance or arrogance, those in charge seem to have forgotten the wisdom that Maya Angelou articulated: *"Elimination of illiteracy is as serious an issue to our history as the abolition of slavery."* Unfortunately, it seems as if many in academia are uninterested in either acknowledging or learning about how their class content and pedagogy reinforce inequity. As challenging as it is, we have to continue to commit to diversifying our faculty and staff, student bodies, and syllabi.

College of education departments have to commit to diversifying their courses, professors, and students. College programs should look to embrace accountability for the impact, or lack thereof, of the students who graduate from their programs. The point of preparing teachers, after all, is for them to teach well.

Our students live in a virtual world. Every protest, instance of police brutality, meme, and news story is available at their fingertips. They are watching, reading, listening, and forming their own ideas and opinions based on the "evidence" of strangers. They are learning how they should be treated or how they should treat others from TikTok, Instagram, and Snapchat. What our students need from their teachers is what students throughout history have needed from their teachers: love, support, and guidance.

Here are ways to show support for our Black students:

- *Some people fail to reckon with the fact that America is a country built on a foundation of slavery, genocide and White supremacy.*

- *Some people fail to reckon with the fact that America still grants real privilege to your Whiteness each and every day.*

- *Some people fail to understand the damage done by having grown up with de facto residential segregation. And yet, racial isolation is a step toward the formation of prejudice and implicit bias.*

- *Some people fail to understand the damage done by having attended schools separated by de facto segregation. And, again, racial isolation is a step toward the formation of prejudice and implicit bias.*

- *Because many people grew up in racial isolation, what they have learned about Black people they learned from a media outlet. And yet, the media, news, sports and entertainment clearly depict Blacks as dangerous stereotypes.*

- *Some people went to racially diverse schools and took "college-bound" classes. Since Black students are disproportionately and unjustly tracked out of these classes, they received dangerous messages about "intelligence" and "race."*

- *When conversations about race or racism cannot be avoided, some people learned to say things like, "I don't see color. I just see people."*

- *Some people went to colleges where Black students were vastly underrepresented. Because higher education remains de facto segregated, they again received false messages about "academic success" and "race."*

- *Some people studied education in college. And yet, even at the institutional level, Black students are underrepresented in teacher prep programs. While trying to learn how to teach Black students, they were isolated from our Black peers.*

- *When conversations about race or racism made some people feel uncomfortable, they think things like, "My family comes from a blue-collar background. We pulled ourselves up by our bootstraps. Every American has that same opportunity."*

- *Some people think that because they choose to work with Black children, problems of prejudice and implicit bias could not possibly apply to them.*

- *Some people refuse to allow news stories about race or racism to come up in their classrooms even when a teenager like Trayvon Martin or Michael Brown were murdered in the streets.*

- *When conversations about race or racism cannot be avoided, some people try to signal their virtue by*

> *working the conversation around to the fact that they voted for Obama.*

- *Some people realize how little they know about race and racism when they first become friends with a Black person. Yet, they think this small exposure makes them automatic experts.*
- *Some people have grabbed the word "woke" and held on to it a little too tightly.*

It's reasonable to assume that right now there are tens of thousands of first-year White teachers across America working in classrooms with Black males. Perhaps you are one of them, and as you read through that list you likely grimaced more than a few items. The good news is that all is not lost. There is still hope. Growing up White is not an insurmountable barrier to being a successful teacher of Black males. It is an obstacle that will take intentionality to overcome, however.

A naïve colorblindness will lead only to continued failure. Address the items on this list and, equally important, add to it. There are far more than 15 ways for educators to do it wrong. Create your list and tell me what I've missed. And then one day, maybe, a Black parent will walk into your classroom, see a White teacher, and smile all on her own before that White teacher says even a word.

Trapped in The Pipeline

Ch. 7

The path to the pipeline often starts very early for Black males who struggle to manage behavioral and/or emotional issues in low-performing schools. In many cases these schools lack the appropriate mental health professionals, highly qualified special education teachers, and trained staff. Federal law requires schools to provide an education for kids with disabilities in an environment as close to a regular classroom as possible. But often, special needs students receive an inferior education, fall behind, and end up with fewer options in life.

For youth with disabilities who end up in jail, education can be minimal, and at times, non-existent, even though federal law requires that they receive an education until age 21. Many often contemplate over the question "is the school-to-prison pipeline a real thing?" From a literal standpoint, absolutely not, the school-to-prison pipeline isn't an actual pathway that leads from the doors of a school right into the not so welcoming waiting arms of the local prison. Instead, this is merely a concept that certain policies are making schools somewhat of a breeding ground for kids to enter the prison system especially young men of color. In recent years, a disturbing shift has occurred in the educational system.

Rather than employ traditional disciplinary measures, such as counseling or detention, when students misbehave, schools are becoming increasingly dependent on suspensions, expulsions, and law enforcement to punish students. Children are being arrested or removed from schools, even for minor discretions, at alarming rates around the country.

Despite being one of the most developed countries in the world, the United States has one of the highest rates of childhood poverty globally. Children born or raised in poverty face a number of disadvantages, most evidently in education. Poverty reduces a child's readiness for school because it leads to poor physical health and motor skills, diminishes a child's ability to concentrate and remember information, and reduces attentiveness, curiosity and motivation. One of the most severe effects of poverty in the United States is that poor children enter school with this readiness gap, and it grows as they get older.

Children feel alienated from society; suffer insecurities because of their socioeconomic status; fear the consequences of their poverty; endure feelings of powerlessness; and are simply pissed off at society's inability to aid in their struggles. Children from lower-income families are more likely than students from wealthier backgrounds to have lower test scores, and they are at higher risk of dropping out of school. Those who complete high school are less likely to attend college than students from higher-income families. For some children, the effects of poverty on education present unique challenges in breaking the cycle of generational poverty and reduce their chances of leading rewarding, productive lives.

One in eleven young black men are incarcerated in America a pathway that many say starts in Pre-K, where students of color are three times more likely to be suspended or expelled than white students, which immeasurably increases their chances of entering the juvenile justice system. Black males are a demographic that continues to be misunderstood in public schools and America.

Black males learning styles and social skills are often misconstrued as being defiant. imagine coming from a destitute home life with constant chaos. And then you walk into a classroom with a myriad of rules and you are expected to shut your mouth and sit still in a desk for hours learning about something that to your understanding, is absolutely extraneous. In most cases, not going to happen.

Black males are not raised with the understanding of how to be socially accepted by others. They are raised with the understanding that I'm just trying to survive by any means necessary. The catch phrase "only the strong survive" is an understatement when you are a Black male growing up in the hood. The skills that Black males acquire to survive growing up in these inner-cities usually don't translate well into the American classroom.

During my professional developments I usually poll the audience and ask "how many of you were raised under the impression to respect your elders as a child?" The hands fly up. It's usually 90 to 95 percent of the room. Then I say, "these kids today were not raised under the impression to respect their elders. They were raised under the impression you don't let anyone disrespect you."

Which raises the next question, what do they deem as disrespectful? And unfortunately, most educators find out the answer to this the hard way, by trial and error. Some people say that black males are slipping through the proverbial cracks, I say they are being strategically shoved. That lack of learning leads to frustration and eventually higher dropout rates, higher rates of poverty, and, ultimately, higher incarceration rates. High-school dropouts in all demographics have a higher likelihood of incarceration at some point in their lives. The reasons are myriad; however, one of the main issues is economic.

More than likely when Black males drop out of high school they simply just don't have the educational background to generate the income and lifestyles and many of them end up trying to make ends meet which often leads to engaging in different crimes. Over half of Black young men who attend urban high schools do not earn a diploma. Of these dropouts nearly, 60 percent will go to prison at some point. Perhaps there is no real connection between these two statistics, or the eerily similar ones associated with young Latino men. Maybe they are just bad apples, destined to fail academically and live a life of crime (sarcasm)!

Students who are at risk of dropping out of high school or turning to crime need more than a good report card. They need alternative suggestions on living a life that rises above their current circumstances. For a young person to truly have a shot at an honest life, he or she has to believe in the value of an education and its impact on good citizenship.

The school to prison pipeline is an unintended byproduct of the zero-tolerance policy. The zero-tolerance policy was intended to reduce, and if possible prevent, future such incidents through the placement of armed law enforcement in schools. These policy's does not discriminate between minor and major offenses but treats all the same, including minor infractions that could easily be handled more informally by the school administration.

These infractions became criminalized, which resulted in children and adolescents being exposed early to the criminal justice system and becoming labeled as juvenile delinquents. Black and minority children have been disproportionately represented in the school-to-prison pipeline. Research indicates that there is a racial gap, meaning when it comes to whether to discipline a student and how depends on the color of a student's skin.

Black and Brown student's punishment tends to be harsher than White students, even when the offenses committed is the same. Many states allow adolescents to be tried as adults if they meet certain criteria but also allow for discretion in making this decision. Black and Brown kids according to studies, are more likely to be tried as adults than their white peers who commit the same or similar offenses.

Note that students from impoverished backgrounds and dysfunctional family situations are also more likely to find themselves in the school-to-prison pipeline, and that students with learning disabilities or who are LGBTQ are also targeted for more severe discipline than cisgender, white students without disabilities. Does a zero-tolerance policy in schools actually work, or does it create a situation where students become more fearful about what might happen to them? There are several pros and cons to review with this approach.

It was just another normal school day in Newtown, Connecticut. When two young men named Dylan Klebold and Eric Harris dressed in trench coats open fire on students that were standing outside of Columbine High School. They then made their way inside the school, where they thoughtlessly begin firing their firearms on victims in the library. Klebold and Harris killed 12 students and a teacher and wounded more than

20 others. Shortly after the two teens committed suicide. At the time, this was the worst high school shooting in U.S. history.

It prompted a national debate on gun control and school safety. In the aftermath of the shootings, many schools across America enacted "zero-tolerance" rules regarding disruptive behavior and threats of violence from students. Columbine High School reopened in the fall of 1999, but the massacre left a scar on the Littleton community.

Horror Story #1: Forgotten Gun.

In early May, Kenny Gappa, 17, a senior at Cannon Falls High School in Minnesota, was voted "Outstanding Senior" by the local Future Farmers of America chapter. A week later, he had been suspended for the rest of the school year and barred from graduation ceremonies. School officials had found a small-caliber rifle and ammunition in Gappa's pickup truck. He used them for squirrel hunting and had forgotten they were there.

Horror Story #2: Helping Grandma.

Taylor Hess's grandmother had a stroke and was moved to assisted living, the 16-year-old varsity swim team star loaded some of her things into his pickup and took them all to Goodwill. Well, almost all. He didn't spot a 10-inch-long bread knife that had fallen on to the bed of the pickup. Unfortunately, officials at his high school in Hurst, Texas, did. Hess was expelled for a year.

Horror Story #3: Don't Hesitate.

Keith Post, 10, a fifth-grader at Pyles Elementary School in Stanton, California, had a spotless discipline record and had earned several citizenship awards when he dutifully turned in a pocketknife a friend had found in the school cafeteria one day in April. School officials suspended him for five days for possession of a weapon because he didn't turn the two-inch-long knife in right away he had waited two hours, afraid his teacher might think it belonged to him.

Horror Story #4: Taking Drugs.

Despite having a bad cold, Dennis Sattley, 15, insisted on going to school. His father gave him a bottle of Symtec throat spray and a bottle of Eckerd's brand Complete Cold Relief pills. When school officials found out, they suspended the ninth-grader a solid A/B student for 10 days since the medications violated the drug policy at Space Coast Junior/Senior High in Port St. John, Florida.

Horror Story #5: Finding Drugs.

After finding a bag of pills on the grounds of Pensacola High School in Florida, sophomore Teresa Elenz hesitated to turn them in because she thought school officials would think they were hers. Another student reported the find anyway and Elenz, who is in the International Baccalaureate program for high-achieving students, found herself facing expulsion. After a legal battle, she was suspended for a month. The bag contained sinus medication and pills for seizures and relaxing muscles.

Horror Story #6: Dangerous Weapon.

Three 13-year-old boys at North Valley Middle School in La Salle, Colorado were fascinated by a 2 ½-inch-long laser pointer one of them had purchased at a local store and brought to school. School officials saw the laser toy as a "dangerous weapon" and suspended all three boys for a year. One of the students, Mitch Muller, now attends what his mother calls "jail school" with students who brought real weapons to school.

Horror Story #7: Drug Sweep.

A drug search at the Wagner Community School in South Dakota led to students being confined to their classrooms for several hours while a police dog sniffed around classrooms and students, some as young as six years old. According to court papers, the police dog became unleashed in a kindergarten class and chased students, causing some to cry and at least one to wet his pants.

Horror Story #8: Forbidden Kiss.

An alert vice principal spotted the violation on October 17 in the hallway at Union Grove High School in McDonough, Georgia: Senior James Maurice was planting a single kiss on the forehead of his girlfriend. As a result of that "inappropriate contact," Maurice was suspended for two days, which meant the starting varsity linebacker was barred from playing in the homecoming football game. According to principal Rodney Bowler, kissing and hugging excessively distracts students from academics.

Horror Story #9: No Talking.

A sixth-grade teacher Mary Bond banned all conversation between boys and girls at Peterson Elementary School in southern Oregon as "a preventative measure" after she noticed students showing public signs of affection during lunch break.

Horror Story #10: Sexual Harassment.

When a girl refused Sal Santana II's request to be his girl-friend, the 12-year-old stuck out his tongue at her. When school district officials learned of the incident, Santana was suspended for sexual harassment.

Horror Story #11: Verbal Harassment.

While playing a game during recess, a sixth-grader in Grand Junction, Colorado had his ball called out of bounds by another student. He said that the call was "gay," thinking the word meant "dumb." He was suspended for two days for saying hurtful things, which his principal regarded as a form of harassment.

Horror Story #12: Deadly Missile.

Police at Palm Beach County Public Schools arrested a 14-year-old student and charged him with "throwing a deadly missile," a second-degree felony. The "deadly missile" was an egg the student was carrying in his pocket. Instead of throwing it, he found himself being handcuffed, read his rights, and led away by police.

Horror Story #13: No Splashing.

A sixth-grader in Inverness, Florida didn't stop when his teachers told him not to jump in rain puddles. He did stop when a police officer at the school took him into custody, charged him with a misdemeanor, and held him in a jail cell for more than two hours.

Supporters of zero-tolerance feel that if students violate school polices then they should receive consequences for their actions. Some people might think these actions are extreme but others say it can also serve as a deterrent for future offenders who might be thinking about committing the same infraction. The reality is that the modern-day legal system takes a zero-tolerance approach in most cases as well. It doesn't matter why you broke the law in most circumstances.

Law enforcement is only concerned with the fact that you broke the law. If you are speeding because you're running late for work I doubt the police officer really cares about your reasoning and you will most likely be ticked. Being delayed might cause you to get fired since you are violating company policy for being late. Even if you can save your employment, there is a good chance that you won't get paid for the time spent dealing with the officer.

Zero-tolerance in a perfect world would aid with reducing school bias because zero-tolerance policies require administrators to respond accordingly regardless of the students race, gender, class, or sexual orientation. There are far too many stories of students receiving leniency because they are smart, have parents involved with the district, or have money that can help them to get out of trouble.

The reality of the modern legal system is that it takes a zero-tolerance approach to sentencing in most situations as well. It doesn't matter why you broke the law in most situations. Law enforcement is only concerned with the fact that you violated the expectations of society. If you are speeding because you're running late for work, you'll probably get a ticket. That delay in receiving the ticket might cause your boss to fire you since you violated company policy too.

Even if you can save your employment, there is a good chance that you won't get paid for the time spent dealing with that situation. Zero tolerance helps to reduce favoritism in schools. Because a zero-tolerance policy requires administrators to act in the same way toward any student who violates the rules covered by this approach, then there is a reduction in favoritism present in the school.

Let's be real, almost anything can be perceived as a weapon with intent. Critics often put zero tolerance policies at schools on blast because there can be some confusion as to what constitutes a weapon. The reality of violence is that almost anything can be turned into something that could harm someone else. Rubber bands might seem like a silly item that is non-threatening, but elastic band injuries are fairly common.

A family in Naperville, IL even sued the school district there because of an eye injury sustained on campus by one. It is important to remember that if a student is bringing items to school, there is intent in that action. Zero tolerance policies are based more on the intent to use an item than the actual product. That's why you can see suspensions sometimes for nail clippers or rubber bands.

There are also times when it seems that everyone involved lacks just a little common sense. A student in the fourth grade had kiddy crush on a young girl in his class. So, he decided to express his feeling via a lover latter. The fourth-grader in Florida drew a small picture that said he "loved her," and then said that she was pretty and cute. The boy went on to say that he liked her hair because it "wasn't sloppy."

He was threatened with sexual harassment charges. The administrators of the school determined that the note was not wanted and prompted inappropriate teasing from the other kids. Common sense must be part of a zero-tolerance policy, but unfortunately, these rules tend to create an over-reaction by the adults in that situation.

Anthony Ruelas was a 15-year-old and attending school in Killeen Texas. One day out of the blue one of his peers begin having an asthmatic attack in class. The teacher was waiting to receive an email from the nurse to determine what she should do. Ruelas upset because nothing was happening to help his classmate he swore at the teacher and carried the girl to the nurse's office. Anthony Ruelas was suspended for two days because he refused to follow the directions from his teacher. Situations like this occur all of the time.

Diane Tran is a straight A honor student working two jobs to help her mom support her siblings. Her job created a situation where she had too many unexcused absences. The honor student was arrested for truancy and held for 24 hours for missing school despite her grades. Those charges were eventually dropped.

Zero tolerance policies were created to prevent school shootings because they gave school districts some leverage in sending home students caught with a deadly weapon on campus. Now that these rules can apply to various situations where a perceived threat takes place, more disruptions to the learning environment occur because of their enforcement sometimes.

That's not to say that there isn't a place for this approach in some situations. Students deserve to have a safe place to learn that is relatively free from disruptions. It is also important for us to remember that kids will joke about things all of the time. They will make questionable decisions sometimes because of the way that their brains develop while growing up. Zero tolerance makes sense when there is an intent to hurt someone else, whether that action occurs with a gun, a nail clipper, or a child's fists. It may not be the correct approach to take when that intent is missing

Ending the School to Prison Pipeline: Calling the police should be a last resort in education, not the first response. At least two-thirds of American high school students attend a school with a police officer, according to the Urban Institute that proportion is higher for students of color. There has been a national push to remove police officers from security positions inside schools. School systems in Minneapolis, Milwaukee, Denver, Portland, and two districts in the Bay Area have all moved to suspend or phase out ties with police. Jesse Hagopian, a teacher and activist in Seattle, says removing police from schools has been a key demand for years.

"There's just so much research that shows that they aren't making our kids safe." Data shows that schools with cops are more likely to refer children to law enforcement, including for non-serious violent behaviors.

In 43 states and the District of Columbia, Black students are more likely to be arrested than other students while at school, according to an analysis by the Education Week Research Center. "And there's been horrific acts of police violence in schools," Hagopian adds. He points to two separate incidents captured on body cameras in the fall semester of 2019.

One officer in Florida put a 6-year-old girl in handcuffs as she sobbed. Another in New Mexico was shown shoving an 11-year-old girl against a wall. Both students were Black. "And what is happening in schools around the country," says Hagopian, "is, instead of figuring out how to help that student who's having a difficult time by having counselors, we meet these kids with force." This all adds up to what Monique Morris calls the criminalization of Black students. "The presence of police in schools, I believe, is fueled by a dehumanization of children of color, which suggests that there needs to be a constant surveillance of these children in schools."

Morris is the author and she says new research shows that police in majority white and affluent schools are more likely to think of their job as protecting the school from outside threats, such as shootings. But in schools that were lower-income and majority students of color, they are instead looking at the students themselves as threats. "For children of color, we see that this leads to a hyper-criminalization and a way that people perceive them to be criminal, even if they are just being children," Morris explains.

School resource officer programs began in the 1950s in Flint, Mich., as a form of community policing and to strengthen ties between young people and police, says Mo Canady of the National Association of School Resource Officers. They grew quickly starting in the 1990s amid fear about school shootings. The U.S. Department of Justice has funded these programs to the tune of tens of millions of dollars, expanding its support after the Parkland, Fla., school shooting in 2018.

Federal data analyzed by the American Civil Liberties Union shows millions of students, especially students of color, attend schools that have police officers, but no nurse or school psychologist. In the past, parents have largely supported the presence of armed officers in schools, and until recently so have teacher unions.

That changed recently when the American Federation of Teachers, one of the country's largest teacher unions, passed a resolution calling for the separation of school safety and policing. There are dozens of documented incidents in the past decade where a resource officer tasered, pepper sprayed, injured or otherwise used force on a student.

Mo Canady of NASRO argues this is a problem of training. When properly trained by his organization, he says SROs can prevent violence and juvenile arrests while building positive relationships. "When these relationships are built the way they should be, then we wind up with students sharing information with SROs. We wind up with parents of students sharing information. And sometimes that information helps us to stop a potential act of violence before it ever, ever occurs."

Still, research doesn't definitively show SROs are effective at improving school safety. The good news, say Morris and Parris, is that there are evidence-based alternatives. These include restorative justice programs, a program called Positive Behavioral Interventions and Supports, and having mental health counselors and other support staff available when students are acting out.

Do Away with Standardized Test: Low standardized test scores can result in schools losing funding and even being shut down entirely. But reliance on standardized tests has also been shown to contribute directly to the school-to-prison pipeline. When classrooms are reduced to "test prep centers" where success is determined primarily by test scores, students are more likely to disengage from their education altogether, according to a study by Fairtest.

Also, high school exit exams have been linked to increases in school dropout and juvenile incarceration rates. "We're not judged (as teachers) by how well we develop the individual (student), we're judged on how well we can prepare these kids to take these math and language-arts tests," said Sergio de Alba, a sixth-grade teacher in Los Banos, Calif. "We need to invest in the whole student... It needs to be about growing as an individual."

Provide More College and Career-Prep: Being unprepared for life after high school can have dire consequences for students, leading to dropout and affecting college and job retention rates. Yet only about half of high school graduates complete a college-prep or career-readiness course, according to a recent study by The

Education Trust. When these resources aren't offered at school, students from disadvantaged backgrounds without good support systems at home are less likely to pursue a higher education or identify career opportunities.

"I believe if students start to feel they have a purpose or goal they want to attain and are educated on how to achieve that, they will more likely pursue a higher education, whether that is community college, university or a vocational program," said Stefanie de la Cruz, a college and financial aid counselor for the Merced Union High School District.

Mental Health Professionals: We should increase social workers and mental health professionals in our schools in underprivileged areas all over the nation, there's an epidemic of mental health issues and home life issues that contribute to negative outcomes. Increasing the number of mental health professionals in inferior schools will have a dramatic effect on student success.

Furthermore, social workers make all the difference in the world for children who suffer from substandard conditions at home. This is essential because problems at home will inevitably come into the school. So, one of the best ways to ensure that children have a solid emotional framework from which to learn is to make sure that their home lives are safe and secure.

Reduce Classroom Size: As stated in the stress trap chapter we have to reduce classroom sizes. Teachers can only be expected to control so many children. In truth, class size is one of the single most effective ways to improve outcomes for children. We shouldn't be surprised when, in a class of 38 students (or more!), there are rampant examples of children acting out. This can take so many different forms, from violence to pulling away socially.

This is one of the biggest contributors to the school to prison pipeline, as when students act out, they are often suspended or expelled. One can hardly blame a teacher for sending the worst of their 40-student classroom to the office for administrative action just simply to allow the rest of the students to get a decent chance at an education. However, this approach is very short-sighted and only serves to make the issues worse.

Practice Restorative Justice: Restorative justice is such an important concept that too few people are aware of in criminal justice reform. It derives from a fundamentally different philosophy from "rules are broken; thus, perpetrators must be punished." Instead, it takes the approach that all parties involved are people, that when infractions occur, there are responsible parties, and part of the perpetrator's responsibility is now to help restore whatever was lost by the infraction.

By relying on restorative justice in schools, what you end up with is an opportunity for a child to see what they have done not simply in terms of stealing or destruction of property, but more so in the light of the person that their actions harmed. Creating situations in which empathy is the solution has shown to yield positive results. It's a practice that humanizes the victim and the perpetrator to one another. It lets them know that their actions do not happen in a vacuum, rather everything they do affects someone else. And it's through this practice that real change happens.

Money, Money, Money: Many people read pieces like this and ask, "well, it sounds great, but where will the money come from?" Usually, solutions are developed independently of funding. Think about the microwave oven. Initially, it was prohibitively expensive for most households. Over time, the cost has come down, and they are now a regular appliance in almost any home. Similarly, many of these ideas are new.

They will be expensive at first. Yes, this will be a hurdle. But, ask yourself, what's the cost that we're already paying today? How expensive is it to house a person in jail versus that same person having a job, housing themselves, paying taxes, and contributing to their local community? We have to find the money somewhere. Over time, it will get cheaper. But the cost today is one in human lives, suffering, and a life that is below that of what we owe ourselves as Americans. Ending recidivism begins with preventing people from going to prison in the first place. And that starts with the schools.

Trapped in the Gaps

Ch. 8

The achievement gap, the learning gap, the attitude gap, the equity gap, the digital gap, the Black achievement gap, the skills gap, the motivation gap, the environmental gap, the communication gap, the readiness gap, the racial gap and so on. Creating true equity should be the objective of educational reform in America. However, that is an enormous and complex task.

We have to aggressively address these gap(s) one classroom, one student, one district at a time. Educational leaders in the 21st century is confronted with the challenging task of reforming current practices that continue to contributed to these "gaps," in which underserved students, students of color, students with disabilities, students in foster care, transient students, and many other disadvantaged groups, are less likely to succeed in reading, among other skills crucial to their success later in life. To close these gaps, the focus needs to shift from equality (treating every student the same) and replace that with equity (ensuring every student has the resources and attention they need).

Simply put, a learning gap is a disparity between what a student has actually mastered and what is expected at a particular grade level. Students can have a learning gap in just one subject area or across the board.

A student's education builds on previous concepts like building blocks. If a student is missing foundational blocks at the bottom, they can't keep building. It often turns into a snowball effect, becoming a bigger problem the longer it goes without a remedy.

Teachers have a lot of content to cover, and sometimes the class needs to move on to the next chapter. If a learner didn't really "get it" there's a good chance that any future concepts that rely on understanding this knowledge are going to be even more difficult to grasp. Teachers have the unique ability to go back and revisit previous topics and subjects that weren't clear, working one on one at the student's pace. As the learner gains clarity into concepts that were not understood previously, the gaps in their learning will gradually begin to close. Learning is constantly about moving forward and building upon previous knowledge, so it's incredibly important for learners to have a firm academic foundation in all subjects.

These gaps are often compounding. Its unquestionably important to address an identified learning gap. If left unaddressed, it can increase the chances that a student will struggle academically and negatively impact their confidence and mental health. It's also important to address the distinction between a learning gap and an achievement gap. An achievement gap means an inequality in educational opportunities whereas a learning gap is focused on what a student should know by a certain point but doesn't. Some may use these terms interchangeably, but they require different remedies to address.

According to the National Assessment of Educational Progress, an achievement gap occurs when "one group of students (e.g., students grouped by race/ethnicity, gender) outperforms another group, and the difference in average scores for the two groups is statistically significant." While achievement differences between demographics are often in the spotlight, there can also be gaps between students with disabilities and those without. Evidence for the achievement gap is most commonly found in dropout rates, test scores, college enrollment rates and other measurements of success in schools.

These gaps have persisted historically, and the turbulence of recent years likely isn't helping. According to a McKinsey & Company report, the educational disruptions caused by the COVID-19 pandemic, including online learning, school closures and teacher shortages, have also had a severe effect on test scores and other educational outcomes. While each student's learning gaps are unique, there are five main types of learning gaps. Regardless of the method of learning, whether in person or online, all five types of learning gaps are seen.

1. ***Skills gaps*** – *A student lacks the practice and mastery of necessary skills.*
2. ***Motivation gaps*** – *A student lacks the motivation or desire to learn the concepts.*

3. **Knowledge gaps** – *A student does not know or lacks exposure to correct information.*
4. **Environmental gaps** – *A student does not have access to a conducive learning environment.*
5. **Communication gaps** – *A student lacks clear communication of concepts or expectations.*

Here are some steps we as educators can take to help close learning gaps:

Normalize Getting Help

Create a safe space where students feel comfortable sharing their concerns is an important step in closing learning gaps. This is because we can't help students that we don't even know need the help. And no one wants to feel like they are struggling alone.

Form Authentic Connections

Part of creating an environment in which students feel comfortable coming to you is forming a connection with them. It is essential to cultivate a classroom community in which learners feel connected to their teacher and peers.

Use Classroom Technology

Utilizing technology-based activities in the classroom makes learning more interactive and engaging for students. Programs like Canvas or Google Classroom can also ensure that all educational activities are contained in one location that is accessible whether the student is at home or school. Additionally, technology can make lessons more accessible for students with different learning styles as well as students with disabilities.

Make It Part of Your Professional Development

Learning never stops for a teacher. And the more you know about learning gaps, the better you'll be at addressing them. Joining teacher networks, taking classes, and attending conferences can help you stay plugged into the most recent developments in addressing learning gaps. It will also give you a community of other teachers who are facing the same challenges. It's not always a simple or quick fix to close learning gaps, so the support can be great for morale.

Read, Read, and Read Some More!

It is irresponsible to effectively discuss and impossible to empathize with others on a topic that you are not educated on yourself. Because of this, the charge is to read as much as possible. Stay up on current events from more than one platform. Find journalists you trust to report the news without bias. Read history, more than what you were taught in school. If you want to quote Martin Luther King Jr., Maya Angelou, or Colin Kaepernick, then read about them. Know their story, their sermons, their plight; understand their platforms. Read books about race by Black authors. Along with nonfiction, read fiction by Black authors, featuring Black characters. Get your hands-on stories that your Black students can relate to and see themselves in, stories that you can use to connect with them.

Redecorate So All Students Are Represented.

Add representation, diversity, and inclusion to your classroom walls. Your students need to see themselves and their classmates when they look around the room. Make sure your posters include children of all skin tones and abilities. Add diversity to your digital classroom. Do you have athletes, scientists, inventors, historical figures, and authors highlighted? If so make sure to highlight Black athletes, scientists, inventors, etc. Studies show that this simple step can help with the development of children's implicit bias (our unconscious attitudes and stereotypes that affect our actions and beliefs). When all students are equally represented in the classroom decor we are making the statement that directly affects how kids see themselves and others.

Diversify Reading Lists and Classroom Libraries.

In the same way that adding diversity to your classroom decor is important, adding it to your bookshelves is just as, if not even more, important. Students need to see themselves in literature. They need to meet characters that they relate to. But more than that, Black students need to be introduced to literature that tells stories about more than just overcoming hardship. They need to be the main character in a story surrounded by other Black characters.

Be Intentional

Black students in predominantly White school settings carry invisible loads that we can't all relate to. When discussing slavery or the Civil Rights Movement, they catch the quick glances of their peers who feel guilty discussing the topics in front of them. They feel the shift in the mood of the class when the answer to the question about why Tom Robinson was found guilty in To Kill a Mockingbird is "because he was Black." They know that as Black students they are four times more likely to be disciplined than White students, and it is very clear to them that 80% of teachers in America are white. As teachers, we need to get uncomfortable with our intention. It is our responsibility to call out stereotypes, to work to dismantle the systematic racism within our buildings and to do whatever it takes to meet the needs of Black students.

Trapped in Black Skin

Conclusion

America is at a critical crossroads. The nation faces the challenge of fulfilling its promise as an inclusive democracy for all, or, continuing as a society crumbing from the weight of anachronistic beliefs and behaviors that concentrate power, wealth and resources in the control of a few.

To be male, poor, and Black is to confront, on a daily basis, a deeply held racism that exists in every social institution. No other demographic group is fared as badly, so persistently and for so long as Black males. Today's educational system is overwhelmed, overburdened and utterly unprepared to educate these Black males. Less than three percent of the nation's teachers are Black males. That's a hard but real pill to swallow.

"Ignorance of each other is what has made unity impossible in the past. Therefore, we need enlightenment. We need more light about each other. Light creates understanding, understanding creates love, love creates patience, and patience creates unity."
~ Malcolm X

We have to come to grips with the fact that representation matters. Black males need to have people that look like them in front of the classroom. When kids see educators that look like them, it gives them the ability to see what they have the possibility to become. In many cases, school systems are not designed for Black males to feel valued or welcomed. The cultural aspects of public schooling are drastically different than what many of our Black male's experience outside of school. And so, we have to really think about how do we address that.

The other components of why the experience for Black males is different: the curriculum. Here in America we have a Eurocentric curriculum. That doesn't center around the experiences of Black Americans and ignores the histories and contributions that ethnic minorities have made to predominantly White countries. Eurocentricity is seen as the sugar-coating of information presented to children. When Black males lack a sense of belonging, they're going to struggle regardless of what their gap may be. That's where you begin to see young, immature minds trying to make decisions for themselves that are well beyond their comprehension.

Black males, more than any other group of male children in this society, are asked to surrender their childhoods at early ages in order to pursue an elusive patriarchal masculinity. Often this demand is made by a dysfunctional single mother who has had all her expectations of being cared for and protected by a patriarchal male shattered; her disappointing father, a deceiving lover, both are part of her abandonment issues. She then projects them onto her son who she hopes will fulfill all her desires...

Redefine Masculinity: If we want to successfully help Black males we need to teach them to be strong without being violent. We need to redefine masculinity and male strength and demonstrate healthier forms of them. In 1920, 90% of Black youth had their fathers in the home because while many were illiterate, they worked on farms. In 1960, 80% had their fathers at home. While many were illiterate, they worked in factories. Today, the figures have dropped to a meager 28%.

Their Black males' goal in life is often to be successful so that they can provide for their mother. Yet their mother may be the person who constantly told them they were bad or destined to be a failure even as she expressed affection. Bradshaw points out that calling children "bad throughout their first seven years is abusive and does damage to their self-worth" and *"spanking and punishing them for being bad causes them shame."* The black male child who is shamed feels flawed and defective. *Those feelings are no doubt compounded as he receives the message from mainstream culture that black men are monsters.*

Imprisoned by Illiteracy: Only 12% of Black males are proficient in reading by 8th grade. If this was the case for White males, the media would categorize this as an epidemic and a national security risk. If a Black male is not proficient in reading by the 4th grade, he will only have a 20% chance of graduating from high school on grade level. I keep naively thinking that America would realize it's more cost efficient to teach Black males literacy, than it is to incarcerate them at $38,000 per inmate per year, with a recidivism rate of 85%. I believe literacy is the civil rights issue of this century. How can Black males be economically competitive illiterate?

Many schools reduced their emphasis on phonics. Other schools believe in social promotion, which explains how Black males are in high school with 4th grade reading and math scores. Can you imagine how Black males feel being in high school illiterate? This explains why many are placed in special education, suspended and dropout. Over 50% of Black males in special education are there because they are deficient in reading.

These are hard facts but ones that have to be faced. The educational system has to consider Black males experiences through the lens of "intersectionality," a framework pioneered by Kimberlé Crenshaw for examining how identities can combine to create specific nodes of disadvantage. Intersectionality points to the need to see individuals in the context of a wide range of identities, rather than in simple binary terms, such as male or female, black or white or gay or straight. This can highlight the position of "multiply-burdened" groups, as Crenshaw puts it.

On many social and economic measures, Black men fare worse not only than white men, but white and Black women. Part of the cause is that Black men are "uniquely stigmatized," according to studies of implicit bias conducted by political scientists Ismail White and Corrine McConnaughy: more than 40% of white respondents rank "many or almost all" Black men as "violent." White men are less than half as likely to be described in this way, at about the same rates as for Black women, while white women are very unlikely to be labeled as violent.

It's no surprise, then, that Black men are also more likely to be stopped by the police, more likely to be frisked, more likely to be arrested, more likely to be convicted, and more likely to be killed by law enforcement. As Rashawn Ray, a Rubenstein Fellow at Brookings argues, "Black men have a different social reality from their black female counterparts," he writes. "The perceptions of others influence black men's social interactions with co-workers and neighbors and structure a unique form of relative deprivation. In this regard, the intersectionality framework becomes useful for illuminating Black men's multiplicities and vulnerabilities."

Given the weight of evidence on the specific, and unique plight of Black males, general policy recommendations will not suffice. Breaking the cycle of intergenerational disadvantage for Black males requires first a deeper understanding the gendering of their race and the racialization of their gender and second, a battery of specifically tailored policy interventions.

For White Teachers Who Teach Black Males: We all live in a culture that has deep roots in white supremacy and oppression. However, in a world where the majority of public-school students are minorities, often in highly segregated schools, and most of their teachers are white, white teachers have a special responsibility to educate themselves so that they can be the teacher their students need. Let's start by addressing the elephant in the room why I am talking only to white teachers? Isn't that racist?

(Hold that question, because I want you to ask yourself that same question again after you've read thought the next few paragraphs, and see if you can understand why.)

I'm specifically addressing white educators because around 83% of teachers in the U.S. are white. Conversations about race are super prevalent right now and for many white people, it feels like stepping into a minefield. They have literally no idea what to say, or feel like they don't understand the history of people of color enough to contribute much to the conversation. Or, they say something they think is totally valid but inadvertently offend people of color in the discussion. Or get their own feelings hurt because they feel "attacked," vowing to never, ever enter another conversation about race again.

Don't Be Afraid to Talk About Race: The first thing that white teachers in majority Black schools need to do is to start talking about race even when that makes them uncomfortable. Remember: It is okay to talk about race. It is okay to name the things that make majority Black schools different from majority white schools. Pretending these differences don't exist makes it impossible for educators to have an impact on the opportunity gaps that exist between white students and students of color.

Listen More Than You Talk: Especially if you are new to a school, you need to get the lay of the land first. Listen and learn all that you can before contributing uninvited to conversations about the way race may impact your school. When your Black colleagues speak in faculty meetings, in casual conversations, in the teacher's lounge, listen to what they are saying. What do they think about what children should be learning? How do they view school policies? What do their lives look like and how does race impact them on a daily basis?

The most valuable group for you to listen to is your students. Learn from them what their lives are like. What does their home environment look like? What do they like to do? What do they think about their neighborhood? If you ask them, they will even tell you what they think about school, the curriculum, and what qualities they value in their teachers. This isn't to say you should never add your input. When you, acknowledge that your life experience looked completely if they did. Contribute your thoughts to the conversation without speaking for or over people of color.

Reject the White Savior Complex: The idea of a "white savior" is the trope of some white teachers, often a woman, coming into a space primarily made up of Black kids and "saving" them; from poverty, disaster, violence, etc. This narrative is problematic because it assumes that Black children are broken and a white person needs to come in and "fix" them. Because this narrative is everywhere, including news, books, and movies, and some would even say the bible. It has become a part of our societal narrative as well. As white teachers, you need to counter this narrative.

Be Authentic: Building relationships with students is key for all educators. It is an especially important step in breaking down stereotypes. By getting to know each child as an individual, you are less likely to rely on stereotypes to fill in the gaps. Building relationships with students of color in predominantly non-white schools as a white teacher comes with a particular set of challenges. Some students may be slower to trust new teachers due to seeing a high turnover rate, particularly of white teachers, in the past. They may keep you at a further distance for the first few months, watching to see how you treat them and whether you seem like you'll stick around.

Another challenge some teachers face is feeling that their students have different interests than them. Some feel that they have to pretend to like hip hop or basketball to relate to students. Students can smell that kind of "fakeness" from a mile away. Instead, focus on being authentic with students. Let them get to know the real you even if you prefer country music and gardening over what you think they like.

Why? You'll find there are some students who'll surprise you, and are into the same things. You'll still be able to find common ground with your students. And they will appreciate you for not being fake. You are not "just" a white teacher. There are many aspects of your identity that you *do* have in common with your students, and living as your full authentic self in the classroom is what will help you form the strongest bonds.

Remember That: Racism is not necessarily about holding hate in your heart toward other people or consciously believing you are superior because you're white. 99.9% of people do not describe themselves as racist because they think that means being a Neo-Nazi or KKK member. However, the racism you keep hearing people talk about these days is far more than some limited dictionary definition, and we need to look at the bigger picture. Racism is about contributing to or looking the other way in the face of acts or systems that marginalize people of color. Racism is a systemic issue. So, if you are complicit in policies and systems that are oppressive to people of color, you are contributing to racism in this country.

If you look the other way or deny that these systems exist, you are part of the problem. Just as a man can be married to a woman and still hold sexist beliefs, you can subconsciously hold ideologies of white supremacy even if you have Black friends. You can know in your heart that you don't hate anyone but still contribute to their oppression. You can love Black culture, music, and slang while benefitting from systems that are designed to elevate you above Black people in social status.

The worst thing you can do is take a knee-jerk reaction to any mention of racism and assume it doesn't apply to you. We all have a lot to learn and examine in that area. No white person is exempt. We ALL need to do the work in uncovering and rooting out bias and internalized anti-Blackness.

There Is No Such Thing as Reverse Racism: It's just not possible, because as we've established, racism cannot exist without a history of systemic oppression and marginalization. Racism is rooted in privilege and power. People of color may hold prejudice toward white people or be biased. But prejudice and racism are very different things it's not just semantics. You have to look at which groups of people have historically had the privilege and power in this country in order to fully understand how racism works. Racism is rooted in a system of white supremacy, so it's about more than just how individuals treat one another.

That's a deep topic, but for now, it's enough to know that encountering a student or parent who says something rude to or about you as a white person does not make you a victim of racism. Their actions while unkind and harmful to your relationship may be the result of frustration with white privilege and constant marginalization on a daily basis.

As a white person, you may bear the brunt of that frustration from a couple of individuals on occasion. You are not, however, the victim of reverse racism. There is no systemic oppression happening or larger patterns of mistreatment that are based on you having less power and privilege than people of color. That is why racism does not "go both ways." It goes in one direction: from the group who holds the power and privilege toward the groups who do not.

Always Remember the Rules Are Different: No, you're not imagining this. There are different rules, and this is not a secret. It's because of these systems of power and privilege I explained previously. The rules for survival and success in this country are not the same for all groups of people, and therefore the way different groups of people talk about race is not the same. Don't frustrate yourself by trying to figure out why Black people can say the N word and white people can't.

Focus on trying to understand the bigger issues of privilege and race, and the smaller details like that will make a lot more sense to you later on. When you hear people of color talking about race (or just talking about life in general amongst themselves), the least helpful thing you can do is to try to police their tone or correct the way they express themselves. Instead, accept that their lived experiences are different than yours: they are treated differently and see the world differently. The rules for how to talk and behave for people of color have never been the same as the rules for those who are white.

Bibliography

A Rich Seam, How New Pedagogies Find Deep Learning By: Michael Fullan & Maria Langworthy. January 2014

Beyond the Stereotypical Image of Young Men of Color Minority youth are often portrayed through a distorted lens. But many live counternarratives every day. By David J. Knight

Black Over-representation in Special Education Not Confined to Segregation States. By Joel McNally

Black students-Middle class teachers. By Jawanza Kunjufu

Brown v. Board: When the Supreme Court ruled against segregation May 17, 2023 | by NCC Staff

Can Professional Environments in Schools Promote Teacher Development? Explaining Heterogeneity in Returns to Teaching Experience

COVID-19 and student learning in the United States: The hurt could last a lifetime. By Emma Dorn, Bryan Hancock, Jimmy Sarakatsannis, and Ellen Viruleg

Finn, J. D., & Rock, D. A. (1997). Academic success among students at risk for school failure. Journal of Applied Psychology, 82(2), 221–234. https://doi.org/10.1037/0021-9010.82.2.221

How to Solve the Teacher Burnout Crisis: 10 Strategies. By Chris Balow

Mahzarin Banaji looks at biology of bias. Social psychologist uses fMRIs, other techniques to understand 'mind bugs. By Corydon Ireland

McConnell, A. R., Sherman, S. J., & Hamilton, D. L. (1994). Online and memory-based aspects of individual and group target judgments. Journal of Personality and Social Psychology, 67(2), 173–185. https://doi.org/10.1037/0022-3514.67.2.173

News media offers consistently warped portrayals of black families, study finds. By Tracy Jan December 13, 2017

Operario, D., & Fiske, S. T. (2004). Stereotypes: Content, Structures, Processes, and Context. In M. B. Brewer & M. Hewstone (Eds.), Social cognition (pp. 120–141). Blackwell Publishing.

Overcoming the soft bigotry of low expectations for black males. By: Dr. Terry Stoops

Preventing Double Segregation for Students with Disabilities By: Halley Potter, Kimberly Quick

Ramos, G., & Hughes, T. R. (2020). Could more holistic policy addressing classroom discipline help mitigate teacher attrition? eJournal of Education Policy, 21(1). https://doi.org/10.37803/ejepS2002

Schneider, D. J. (2004). The psychology of stereotyping. The Guilford Press.

Teacher Attrition: Differences in Stakeholder Perceptions of Teacher Work Conditions. By: Randall Davies, Bryan Bowles, Joseph Hanks, Ross A. Larsen, Steve Christensen

The Coddling of the American Mind: How Good Intentions and Bad Ideas Are Setting Up a Generation for Failure
Authors: Jonathan Haidt, Greg Lukianoff

The impact of schoolwide positive behavioral interventions and supports on bullying and peer rejection: a randomized controlled effectiveness trial. Tracy E Waasdorp, Catherine P Bradshaw, Philip J Leaf

The Invented History of 'The Factory Model of Education' By: Audrey Watters

The Trouble with Teacher Turnover: How Teacher Attrition Affects Students and Schools. By Desiree Carver-Thomas & Linda Darling-Hammond

Understanding Bias and the Brain Exploring the neural pathways of prejudice may offer clues to lessening its effect. By Korn Ferry

Wagner, T. (2008). The Global Achievement Gap: Why Even Our Best Schools Don't Teach the New Survival Skills Our Children Need, and What We Can Do about It. New York: Basic Books.

We Need to Be Nurtured, too': Many Teachers Say They're Reaching A Breaking Point. Written by Kavitha Cardoza Published: 19 April 2021

Written in Black & White, Exploring Confirmation Bias in Racialized Perceptions of Writing Skills
Lead Researcher: Dr. Arin N. Reeves

Why Do Teachers Stay? Exploring Teacher Retention in Urban Schools Amanda B. Flentge, Ed.D. Mentor: Bradley W. Carpenter, Ph.D.

Yale Study Finds Signs of Implicit Racial Bias Among Preschool Teacher. By Emma Brown